BOXER

SMART OWNER'S GUIDE™

FROM THE
EDITORS OF
DOG FANCY
MAGAZINE

CONTENTS

Boxer, a Smart Owner's Guide™
part of the Kennel Club Books® Interactive Series™
ISBN: 978-1-593787-65-3. ©2009

Kennel Club Books Inc., 40 Broad St., Freehold, NJ 07728. Printed in China.
All rights reserved. No part of this book may be reproduced in any form,
by Photostat, scanner, microfilm, xerography or any other means, or incorporated
into any information retrieval system, electronic or mechanical,
without the written permission of the copyright owner.

*photographers include Isabelle Francias/BowTie Inc.;
Tara Darling/BowTie Inc.; Gina Cioli and Pamela Hunnicutt/BowTie Inc.*

For CIP information, see page 176.

K9 EXPERT

If you have taken a Boxer into your home from a responsible breeder or a rescue group — or are planning to do so — congratulations! You have fallen in love with one of the most appealing characters in all of dogdom.

The American Kennel Club breed standard describes the Boxer as combining strength and agility with elegance and style.

He'll remind you of the athletic jock you knew at school who managed to score touchdowns on the football field and straight As on his exams. With his heart of gold and easygoing attitude, he was living proof that nice guys can and do finish first, not last. That's the Boxer. Big man on campus; totally cool and down-to-earth; and everyone's likeable bud.

EDUCATION

This breed exhibits curiosity and fearless courage, yet instinctively knows when to tread gently. He is especially patient around the young and the elderly. Many families have fond memories of their children learning to walk by leaning on a pet Boxer.

As the breed standard states unequivocally, character and temperament define the Boxer. Meeting a Boxer for the first time, most people are struck by his dignity, confidence and alert bearing. In the show ring, he is a spirited performer, occasionally silly, but working as one with his human partner. He is animated but under control.

In the words of the breed standard, the Boxer's eyes mirror his moods. Combined with the wrinkling of his forehead, the Boxer possesses one of the most expressive faces you'll ever encounter.

The Boxer's good looks are famous. His short, shiny tight coat hides nothing. This is a spit-and-polish breed when it comes to grooming. The Boxer requires an occasional brushing, along with regular ear cleaning and nail cutting. Wipe his facial wrinkles with a damp cloth to keep them clean.

In the food department, the Boxer is generally considered an easykeeper — healthy with a good appetite.

Early socialization and ongoing training are essential to channel the breed's energy in a positive manner. Boxers are smart and adaptable, but you must provide them with a daily outlet for their exuberance. Cooped up and deprived of exercise, the Boxer can go stir crazy and is inventive in finding unacceptable ways to amuse himself.

Whatever the task, this dog will be your enthusiastic sidekick. Boxers do slow down,

eventually. However, they are in no hurry to grow up. They tend to be perpetual youngsters, greeting each new day with wonder. It's difficult not to smile when you see a Boxer wagging his tail by wagging his entire back end. To appreciate a Boxer fully, you need energy and a sense of humor.

Allan Reznik
Editor-at-Large, DOG FANCY

CHAMP

The affable, people-oriented Boxer possesses a delightful but challenging overabundance of personality, which demands management and patience on the smart owner's part. Exuberant, enthusiastic, active, independent, with a love for clowning, well-bred Boxers have temperaments well-suited for interactive pet owners with high-energy lives.

Knowing the temperament traits of the Boxer and what they will mean to you as a potential Boxer companion are essential before bringing home that jowly mug on four (powerful) legs. To make it easy, we've listed the top Boxer characteristics.

ROUND 1: EXUBERANCE UNLEASHED

Ask any Boxer owner what Boxers are like and chances are you'll hear the word "exuberant" mentioned at least once. "They can be pretty boisterous, and that gets on some people's nerves," says Virginia Zurflieh, a Boxer breeder in Tampa, Fla. "They aren't hyper, but they are certainly enthusiastic."

That natural enthusiasm can be a bonus in the show ring, where having an animated personality makes the Boxer stand out, but it can also be a deterrent in activities, such as competitive obedience. "They really are free spirits," says Wendy Wallner, D.V.M., a Boxer breeder in Loganville, Ga. "Obedience competition can turn into a comedy act when a Boxer decides to take a break right in the middle of a recall [an obedience cue that you use to call the dog toward you] to roll in something that smells good in the middle of the ring, or take a detour to go visit interesting people sitting in the crowd. Then, they come back, do

what you said, and act like it was all part of the routine."

This isn't a mellow, couch-potato dog. Although Boxers are less active than some dogs, they do best with owners who appreciate and can accommodate their natural exuberance and zest for life.

"Even though we spent a lot of time researching different breeds, we were not prepared for the exuberance of a Boxer. It has been an adjustment, but we love our Boxer dearly, and Sable really is such a good dog," says Boxer owner Janet LaGasse from Nashville, Tenn. "But sometimes we think we should have named Sable 'Rambunctious' instead. Of course, she's so cute that she gets away with things."

ROUND 2: FOREVER YOUNG

Boxers calm down once they reach adulthood (at around 3 years of age), but they never lose their playful spirit. "I have a 10-year-old Boxer who still acts like a puppy," Wallner says. "Even in their old age, they are pretty active and stay a lot like puppies right to the end." Boxer owners often laugh about what Wallner calls the "running fit." "Louise gets so excited, she starts running amok, especially on the agility course, dashing through the tunnel a few extra times even though she hasn't been asked to and racing in big circles; I can't help laughing at her," she says. "All I have to do is make a funny sound, and [all 10 of my Boxers] start running as fast as they can in big circles."

Sure, Boxers can be very well-behaved and in perfect control, but watch out for that merry twinkle in their eyes because if anyone proposes a game, a Boxer — no matter what his age — will be more than ready to play hard.

ROUND 3: BUSY BODIES

Boxers are athletic, high-energy dogs with lots of muscle to maintain. They are also intelligent and if you don't keep those brains busy, you'll have a bored buddy. In fact, mental stimulation may be even more important for Boxers than hours of physical exercise. "My Boxers are perfectly content to lie around the house," Zurflieh says. "It's simply a matter of devoting enough time, attention and training to them."

Did You Know? **According to the American Boxer breed standard,** a written description of what an ideal breed should look like, a Boxer's tail should be set high, docked and carried upward.

Satisfy your brainy and brawny Boxer by getting involved in organized activities, such as agility and competitive obedience, or more casual pursuits, such as hiking, walking and mastering tricks. Agility in particular, is a Boxer favorite. Confident enough not to fear the equipment, they also have the strength and flexibility to fly through an agility course with impressive speed, style and grace.

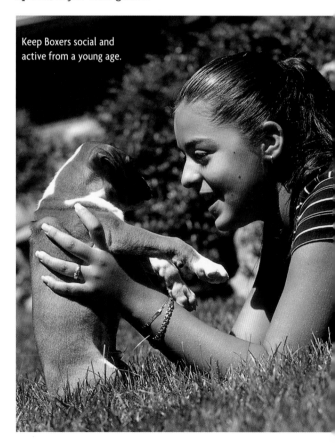

Keep Boxers social and active from a young age.

"Boxers love agility, and they do agility much better than obedience because it's freer and it's fun," Wallner says. "It appeals to the fun side of them."

Boxers' high energy and intelligence mean you must stay one step ahead of them, during activities and at home. Boxers are notorious for foiling your efforts to keep them under control. "I've had [Boxers] who could figure out any kind of latch for any crate or pen in no time. Sometimes they have the door open before you can turn around and walk away," Wallner says. Boxers are good jumpers and may also escape from fenced yards if they are bored and see something fun to chase on the other side of the fence.

ROUND 4: STIMULATION REQUIRED

Because Boxers are strong, curious and need lots of stimulation, a bored Boxer can easily become destructive — especially in puppyhood. Roy, one of Zurflieh's Boxers, shredded the door to the laundry room by peeling off the veneer, strip by strip, down to the plywood underneath. "Then he did it to my kitchen cabinets, but when I placed him in a home where he was the only dog and was doted on all the time, he became the most perfectly behaved dog with the most wonderful temperament," Zurflieh says.

Boxers must constantly be mentally engaged, so training in puppyhood is a must. "My advice is to take your Boxer to obedience class, and don't think one class is going to be the end of the training," Wallner says. "Training is ongoing. You can't get a dog and never do anything with it and expect it to be perfect, to not chew things, to not misbehave, to not be destructive. You have to show them how to be good dogs."

Boxers are very playful and need lots of exercise and stimulation.

Their name may imply that they like to fight, but nothing could be farther from the truth. You could say that they are lovers, not fighters!

Boxer puppies start out small, but they grow into large dogs quickly! That doesn't mean they mature fast, though.

ROUND 5: INDEPENDENCE

Some dogs are clingy and needy — not the Boxer. "They don't crave constant attention; they just want to know where you are," Wallner says. "Boxers are independent and can amuse themselves for hours. They may follow you around the house, but they don't have to be touching you all the time like some breeds."

Boxers' independence is due in part to their heritage as working guard dogs, responsible for alerting their owners to the presence of intruders. That same independence means that they can be a challenge to train. "They are way too independent to fall all over themselves doing what you want," Wallner says. "But, if you make it fun for them, they will learn so fast that it's almost scary."

Within 24 hours of bringing her home, LaGasse taught Sable to ring a bell to go outside. "Every time I took her out, I would ring the bell, take her out, then give her a treat," LaGasse says. "She figured out how to do it on her own in 24 hours. We think that's pretty impressive."

NOTABLE & QUOTABLE

Training the Boxer for competition requires much patience. Not because the dog can't learn, but because she is such a natural clown. The Boxer loves playing to an audience and frequently hams it up at a trial.

— Boxer breeder James Kilman from Grove City, Ohio

The results are in, and here are five great reasons to love the Boxer.

1. Creature comforts: For starters, Boxers can be cuddly. "Boxers love their comfort," says Craig Powell of Catonsville, Md., a member of the American Boxer Rescue Association. "They work best when in charge of the laws of gravity, making sure that the couch or bed stays firmly planted on the floor." Ann Keil, a veteran Boxer breeder and handler from Tiffin, Ohio, agrees. "You've never seen 70 pounds make themselves smaller in your entire life," she says. "They're like giant suction cups."

2. Sensitive souls: These dogs can tune into the feelings of others. "They know what mood their owner is feeling and adjust their actions accordingly," Powell says. "There are many anecdotes of dogs who act happy when their owners are happy and dogs who act low-key when there is sadness or illness in the family."

3. Jerk finders: Boxers have a keen sense of spotting a "bad boy." "One of the things I like about the Boxer as a woman's dog is that he is a very judgmental dog," Keil says, referring to the Boxer's ability to detect a jerk when a woman is on a date.

4. Loyal companions: "The dog is terribly loyal," says Eleanor Linzerholm-Wood of Phoenix, Ariz., a historian with the American Boxer Club. "The Boxer would rather be with his close ones than anywhere else. His first loyalty is to the individuals who are part of his family."

5. Gentle critters: "The Boxer is a gentleman among dogs with short coats," wrote Frau Stockmann in *My Life With Boxers* (Coward-McCawn, 1968). "He not only wants the best food; he wants to be handled in a civilized manner, too. He cannot stand a hard hand or injustice. His real job is to be a house and family dog and be a friend to the children."

ROUND 6: JUMPING FOR JOY

Boxers may be independent, but when it comes to company, their curiosity and love of people get the best of them. Echo will sit nicely by Sue Anne Thompson of Iowa City, Iowa, when visitors drop by — that is until Thompson becomes distracted. Then, Echo will slyly inch toward the new person until she is standing on the visitor's lap, face-to-face with this interesting new human. A few kisses are usually in order, too. "She's so well-behaved until someone new comes over," Thompson says. "It's the one thing I can't seem to train out of her, that need to get right up on people."

"If only everyone could see the sweet, calm, well-behaved dog we see every day around the house," sighs LaGasse when considering Sable's boisterous energy. "But no, when company comes over, all she wants to do is jump. She just can't help getting in your face."

ROUND 7: LOVE, EXCITING AND NEW

Because Boxers are incredibly friendly, people-oriented and readily adapt to new situations, they are easy to place into new homes. A well-screened rescue Boxer is a great choice for people who don't want to deal with puppyhood. "Boxers bond quickly to any new owner who treats them well," Thompson says. "Some breeds bond to one person only, but these guys are great for families because they love everybody." Of course, he who controls the kibble bag might have a slight edge.

Because Boxers adjust to new situations so readily, they make excellent adoptees. Consider a well-screened adult Boxer from a breeder or responsible rescue group.

ROUND 8: ANY FRIEND OF YOURS

Boxers look intimidating, no doubt about it. Their size and natural tendency to bark an alert should scare away would-be intruders, but what if someone actually breaks into your house? Less territorial than some breeds, you can't be guaranteed that your Boxer will do anything more than bark.

"I like to refer to the Boxer as a sensible guard dog," Zurflieh says. "A typical Boxer can differentiate between the guy who approaches your house with a lock pick and a screwdriver, and the neighborhood kid who wanders into your yard through the open gate. You don't have to worry so much about a Boxer nailing your friends or neighbors if they approach your territory because they are so level-headed."

Some Boxers are likely to be friendly to everyone — intruder or not. "Sable may look pugnacious, but she loves everybody she meets," LaGasse says.

"I don't know if any of my Boxers would protect me if it came to that," says Wallner, who has seen rescued Boxers trained to be aggressive. "It really messes them up; Boxers are not attack dogs," Wallner says.

Any Boxer who behaves viciously or bites a human is not exhibiting a Boxer's temperament. "That's not a Boxer," Zurflieh says. "Viciousness is not a trait you train out

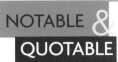
A Boxer needs a lot of interaction with his owner or family along with a great deal of exercise. If ignored, this breed can be imaginatively destructive.
— *Lois Brooks, rescue coordinator from Delaware, Ohio*

of Boxers; it should not be there to begin with. Being dog-aggressive is one thing, but Boxers know the difference between dogs and humans."

ROUND 9: WANNA MAKE SOMETHING OF IT?

When it comes to other dogs, however — especially dogs of the same sex — Boxers are not so likely to get along without incident. Aggression seems to be most problematic between females, although unneutered males can also fight. "Once two Boxers have had an argument, it's never over," Thompson says. "They hold a grudge, and they will be enemies forever and can't be trusted to be together." Anyone who gets in the middle of a Boxer spat risks injury, not because Boxers would attack a person, but because they are so focused on besting their enemy.

Sadie, one of Zurflieh's Boxers, was a wonderful housepet, perfectly housetrained, trustworthy, loving and affectionate, but this show champion had to go to a new family. "I placed her in a pet home because she absolutely would not get along with the other dogs," Zurflieh says. "In a house full of humans, though, she was the most wonderful housepet you could ever imagine."

Many breeders have had to place loving, well-behaved Boxers because they couldn't live with other Boxers. "Witchie gets along with Raider and Tassell, but she hated Beanie with a passion, to the point where it was dangerous living with the two dogs, so I had to place Beanie," Thompson says. "I keep her away from my two female puppies, Echo and Spice, because it could easily happen again."

Zurflieh's Roy wouldn't tolerate her champion male, necessitating his adoption. "I would never have placed him if he could get along with Max, but Max was my old boy," Zurflieh says. "It's something you have to consider."

"I would never, ever place a female Boxer in a home with another female," Wallner says. "That's no way for a pet to live. Sure, there are a few exceptions, but the problem may not surface for a few years, and what are you going to do when it does? It's not worth the great risk."

Boxers also have a highly developed prey drive. Puppies can learn to get along with a family cat if raised together, but Boxers can't be trusted around unknown cats, let alone squirrels, rabbits, birds, waterfowl, even deer. Thompson's first Boxer, Pepper, once ate an entire goose. Zurflieh had a friend who suspected her Boxers were slowly picking off the ducks in her decorative pond. "Boxers aren't the kind of dogs you have to muzzle while walking to and from the show ring, but put a bunch of them together and you've got a dog pack," Zurflieh says.

it's a **Fact** Although traditionally not as popular as other breeds of working dogs, hundreds of Boxers served during World War I and II not only as guard and patrol dogs, but also as messenger dogs, a job that required negotiating mud-slickened, shell-shocked ground during heavy fire to carry messages between troops. The Boxer also transported communications wires, wearing a spool of wire that unwound as the dog ran between units on the battlefield.

Not to say they aren't loyal, but Boxers are easygoing and will love their owners — whoever that person is at the time.

Set at the highest points of the sides of the skull, a Boxer's ears are customarily cropped, cut rather long and tapered and raised when alert. If uncropped, the ears should be of moderate size, thin, lying flat and close to the cheeks in repose, but falling forward with a definite crease when alert.

ROUND 10: DON'T WORRY, BE HAPPY

Best of all, Boxer owners say, Boxers are just plain happy dogs. "Boxers are always happy," Wallner says.

"I think they get their easygoing, nothing-bugs-me temperament from the Bulldogs and Mastiffs originally used to create them," Zurflieh theorizes. Their good-natured spirits can help to soften anyone's wrath upon discovering a chewed shoe or a dinner stolen from the counter.

Of course, that face helps too, adding a certain charm not only to the Boxer's conformation but to the general impression of a Boxer's personality. LaGasse admits that not everyone finds Boxers attractive, but to her they are the cutest dogs around. "She's such a pretty little girl with her little turned-up nose, those big brown eyes," says LaGasse of Sable.

WINNER BY A KNOCKOUT!

By now, you should have a pretty good idea whether a Boxer's temperament will suit your own and your family's temperament and lifestyle. If a Boxer sounds like he would be a perfect match for your family, then enjoy the journey ahead. It's bound to be full of fun. If you've already brought home your Boxer puppy and found this information

eye-opening, consider the benefits of a little extra work. LaGasse got more than she bargained for with Sable, but advises Boxer owners everywhere to work with their exuberant friends and accept them for who they are: "Sable may be a little more active than we expected," she says. "She's a high-energy, exuberant dog, but she is also delightful — so expressive and so loving. We love her cute face, the way she prances on those little white feet, the way she loves everyone unconditionally. You work it out, and it's worth every minute."

Boxers & Kids

Sue Anne Thompson remembers the bare spot on the lawn where Pepper would spend hours playing with the little boy on the other side of the fence in Thompson's Iowa City, Iowa, neighborhood. A similar worn spot on the little boy's side of the fence was testament that the fun was mutual. One side of the fence was littered with children's toys, the other with dog toys.

Being perpetual puppies themselves, Boxers are naturally drawn to children and because they aren't as territorial as some working dogs, they can be a good fit for families. "Boxers don't pick favorites. They love everyone equally, and they just love to play with kids," says Thompson, a Boxer breeder in North Liberty, Iowa.

However, Boxers are strong, boisterous and enthusiastic. Small children could easily be knocked over or injured by a playful Boxer, especially a puppy still lacking in self-control. "Individuals of any breed can be extreme, but generally, Boxers are great with kids," Thompson says. Of course, don't expect your Boxer puppy to act just like that calm, controlled 6-year-old Boxer you met at the dog park. Boxers require training and socialization to develop into friendly and sensible human companions. "Puppies especially are very active," Thompson says.

Sometimes, though, a Boxer may surprise you. Sable had never met a child before, but when the LaGasse family of Nashville, Tenn., took their Boxer puppy to the marina one afternoon, a woman spotted her and called her entire family over to see the dog. "They had a baby barely walking, probably just about 1 year old, and the first thing they did was set the baby down right in front of Sable, the last thing I would have done with a strange dog," says Janice LaGasse.

As soon as the active puppy saw the baby, she lowered herself to her belly. "She crawled over to that baby and licked her on the lower leg," LaGasse says. "Somehow, she knew it was a baby and although she jumps on people in her exuberance all the time, she knew this was a person she couldn't jump on. We were all amazed at how she knew that."

THE BOXER IN BRIEF

This fun-loving, energetic dog will be a playful addition to your family.

COUNTRY OF ORIGIN: Germany

WHAT HIS FRIENDS CALL HIM: Ali, Tyson, Moe

SIZE: 53 to 71 pounds; 23 to 25 inches

COAT & COLOR: The Boxer's coat is short, shiny, smooth and tight to the body. It can be fawn or brindle with a black mask; white markings are not to exceed one-third of the coat.

PERSONALITY TRAITS: Boxers are fun-loving, playful, loyal and affectionate. They may be initially wary with strangers, but they are generally confident enough to make friends easily.

WITH KIDS: Boxers are excellent with children.

WITH OTHER PETS: Boxers do not do well with other pets, especially small animals and dogs of the same sex.

ENERGY LEVEL: These dogs have moderate to high energy levels and crave an active lifestyle.

EXERCISE NEEDS: Daily walks and play sessions are a must to keep these dogs happy, healthy and out of trouble.

GROOMING NEEDS: A weekly rubdown with a bristle brush will keep them clean; occasional baths and nail trims are required as well.

TRAINING NEEDS: These intelligent dogs learn new things quickly and respond well to training.

LIVING ENVIRONMENT: The Boxer can adapt to most living situations as long as he is exercised.

LIFESPAN: 10 to 12 years

Sleek, strong and self-assured, the Boxer is one of several Working Group breeds developed in Germany in the late 19th century. The breed descends from a type of dog found throughout Europe for the past 500 years. A member of the bully breed line, the Boxer's family tree includes almost every recognized breed of the Bulldog type, including the Dogue de Bordeaux and the Bulldog itself.

The Boxer we know today has existed for only the past hundred years or so, but his distant ancestors can be seen in 16th- and 17th-century Flemish tapestries depicting the popular sports of the day: stag and boar hunts led by great dogs capable of taking on and overcoming their dangerous prey. Known as *Spanish Alanos*, the dogs on the tapestries are believed to be ancestors of the Boxer or to share a common ancestor with him.

THREE DOG TYPES

European writings from the 12th to 14th centuries tend to use the word "dogge" to describe all strongly built, shorthaired chase dogs with large heads, powerful muzzles, and strong bodies and teeth. Eventually, three dogge types came to be known: the heavy *bullenbeisser* (bull biter), ancestor of

Did You Know?

A versatile, medium-sized dog, it is generally believed that the Boxer traces her earliest origins back to the Tibetan Mastiff and the massive Molossian Hound, the legendary fighting dog of ancient Greece.

Philip Stockmann, the famous German breeder of Boxers, fretted over the breed's name in his book, *My Life with Boxers*. He bemoaned that this valiant German dog had an English name! The Boxer, we must admit, does have ties to the United Kingdom, and there's more than a little Bulldog in the Boxer's gene pool.

mastiff-type dogs; large hounds derived from *bullenbeisser* and wolf- or deer-hound crosses, which led to the development of the Great Dane; and the small *bullenbeisser*, the progenitor of the Boxer and Bulldog.

The small *bullenbeisser* came from Brabant, an area in northeast Belgium. This type is generally accepted as a direct ancestor of the modern Boxer, and indeed the historical descriptions of the small *bullenbeisser* echo the Boxer look of today. In the book, *The Boxer*, first published in 1939, author John Wagner quotes Hans Friedrich v. Flemming of Leipzig, who wrote in 1719 of the *Brabanter bullenbeisser* that "the ears are clipped while they are still young and also the tail." *Bullenbeissers* are described as fawn or brindle with black masks. White is not mentioned in the breed until after 1830, when a number of English

Bulldogs were brought to Germany, many of which were crossed with the *bullenbeisser*.

Bullenbeissers were valued for their willingness and ability to tackle game from behind and hold it until the hunter arrived for the kill. In the political turmoil of the 19th century, however, many European estates were broken up, and the *bullenbeissers* found themselves out of work. They soon found new employment with butchers and cattle dealers, who found them useful for keeping unruly livestock in line and also with families, who appreciated their guarding abilities. Wagner wrote, "[the *bullenbeisser's*] remarkable intelligence and tractability endeared him to so large a group of individuals that he carried on when so many breeds completely disappeared."

FIGHTING HISTORY

The ancestors of Boxers came about at a time when people were fascinated with "blood sports." The baiting of bulls and bears became a mainstream attraction, and breeds that were strong, agile and fearless were needed to win and to keep the paying audience aroused and entertained.

Fortunately for the Boxer, his ancestors were not ideally suited for this bloody pastime: They were neither agile enough nor small enough to dodge the horns and hooves of the poor captive bull, which passionately was trying to protect itself from the jaws of the dogs. The smaller dogs were quicker and more inclined to fight "head on." These miniature gladiators (weighing approximately 35 to 55 pounds) would excel in the dog pit, battling fellow canines. The "sport" of dog fighting followed swiftly on the heels of animal baiting. In some countries today, including the United States, such heinous sporting still goes on, albeit illegally. By the mid-19th century, bullbaiting and dog fighting were banned in Germany, the Boxer's homeland.

On a more civilized and utilitarian route, the Boxer's ancestors were commonly employed as butcher dogs, for their ability to hold a bull and drive the animal into its pen, should it become unruly. The famous reputation of a dog named "Boxl," used by a butcher in Berlin, is credited for giving the breed its name. The derivation of the word "Boxer" for a purebred dog is ironic because the term "boxl" or "boxel" essentially translates to "mutt"!

In 1894, a famous German breeder of Bulldogs, Friedrich Roberth, was the first to coin the name "Boxer" in print. His article, which ran in a local paper, complimented the Boxer for his intelligence and appearance, ranking the dog higher than any of the other breeds Roberth had owned, which were considerable. He acknowledged, however, that his Boxer female had a cleft palate and loose shoulder, but otherwise impressed all who met her.

He also states that there were no breeders of the German Boxer who were pursuing a serious program, adding that it was rare to get a litter with more than one or two good pups. Roberth's article concluded with a plea for any established, knowledgeable dog person to initiate a club for the Boxer in Germany. As is the case in the dog world today, a new breed is best established by persons already "in the fancy." Roberth

knew that this was the only viable way for a new breed to take hold in Germany.

THE MAN FROM MUNICH

The 19th century could well be described as the century of canine improvement: Many fanciers strove to perfect specific breeds, as opposed to the general types that had previously been known. This pastime was especially popular in the dog-loving countries of England and Germany.

In Munich in the 1880s, a man named Georg Alt imported from France a brindle *bullenbeisser* female named Flora. He bred Flora to an unnamed local dog. The litter she produced included a fawn-and-white male called Lechner's Box, who was bred back to Flora. One of their puppies, Alt's Schecken, was bred in 1895 to a white bulldog called Dr. Toneissen's Tom and became the mother of the first Boxer registered in the German studbook, *Muhlbauer's Flocki*. Schecken's sister, Alt's Flora II, was bred back to her father, "Box," and produced Maier's Lord, who became the first notable Boxer sire. A high degree of inbreeding continued in the Boxer's early days; this was necessary to stamp the breed with a distinct type.

In 1896, a Boxer club was formed in Munich. Naturally, the founders' first step was to draw up a breed standard, a written ideal of the breed, and much of what they described as their ideal dog remains in the Boxer breed standards of today, although the breed itself has become much more refined. The Boxer as it was first developed became a streamlined form of the *bullenbeisser*.

The new dogs were popular for their courage and guarding ability. Boxers were among the first dogs trained for police work, and they were also known to serve as dog guides. During World War I they were at the front lines, working as messenger dogs, pack dogs and scouts for snipers. The Munich breed club donated 10 Boxers to the war effort. One of those dogs was Rolf v. Vogelsberg; he was the only one of the 10 to return alive.

THE BOXER IN AMERICA

The first Boxer registered by the American Kennel Club was Arnulf Grandenz, in 1904.

Surprisingly, unlike many imported breeds, the Boxer was not popular. Eight years later, in 1912, Mrs. Herbert Lehman, the New York governor's wife, imported one of Rolf's sons, German Sieger Dampf v. Dom, the first Boxer to earn an American Championship title in 1915. Still the breed stirred little interest. The intervention of World War I didn't help matters much. It wasn't until 1932 that the breed had its first Best In

You have an unbreakable bond with your dog, but do you always understand him? Go online and download "Dog Speak," which outlines how dogs communicate. Find out what your Boxer is saying when he barks, howls or growls. Go to **DogChannel.com/Club-Boxer** and click on "Downloads."

Show winner, German Sieger Ch. Check v. Hunnenstein.

"Check was credited with stimulating the first real American interest in the breed," says Boxer expert Billie McFadden of Flemington, N.J. "From 1932 to 1934, he was shown 36 times and won Best of Breed 35 times, placing in the Non-Sporting Group [at that time the Boxer's group] 22 times."

With the breed now firmly established, the American Boxer Club was formed in 1935. World War II interrupted the breed's rise to popularity, but from 1946 to 1956, the Boxer was a star. The first great American-bred Boxer of this period was Ch. Warlord of Mazelaine, the first member of the breed to take BIS at the Westminster Kennel Club Dog Show in 1947. Warlord was a son of Utz, one of the German Boxers who had a profound influence on the breed.

Following in Warlord's pawprints was another Mazelaine dog, Ch. Mazelaine's Zazarac Brandy, who took BIS at Westminster in 1949. He also won an all-breed-record 61 BIS awards — an incredible feat at a time when there were no jet planes to whisk dogs around the country from show to show.

But the greatest Boxer of them all soon took center stage. His name was Ch. Bang Away of Sirrah Crest and no lesser mortal than Frau Friederun Stockmann, the German "mother" of the breed who had produced many of the dogs behind the American lines, christened him the best Boxer in America. In 1951, Bang Away took BIS at Westminster, the third Boxer in seven years to do so, and a year later he broke Brandy's record of 61 BIS wins.

Bang Away was celebrated and called "the immortal champion," says McFadden, who has been involved with the breed since 1966. "He was described as being like a piece of machinery. You just wound him up at the show and you could forget about him."

The Boxer may call Germany his homeland, but his fame and popularity spread in the United States.

Search-and-Rescue Extraordinaire

An earthquake rocked the San Francisco Bay Area Oct. 17, 1989. Jedapay's Jaunty Juba, the first Boxer to be certified as a search-and-rescue dog outside Europe, responded to the disaster with owner Rhonda Dyer of San Jose, Calif. They searched rubble piles alongside other SAR teams. Their efforts helped locate an earthquake fatality in the wreckage of a coffee-grinding company. It was here where Juba's training, which included obedience, tracking and agility, became apparent.

"She walked out onto the top of a roof under which the supports had given away, and as she put her weight on one foot the whole top of the roof folded over," Dyer says, remembering how her heart seemed to stop in mid-beat. "She didn't panic at all. She threw her weight back and just stepped back and stood there and looked over the edge at me. That was the result of all of that agility training."

Two years later, in 1991, the little black brindle and Dyer were again involved in a high-profile search in the aftermath of the Oakland Hills firestorm. Three days passed before the surfaces of the collapsed, burned-out buildings had cooled enough for Juba, who certified in SAR at 18 months, to traverse. Only 3 to 4 inches below the surface the embers remained hot to the touch. Juba's job was to detect human remains from among the piles of charred timbers and unidentifiable objects. She worked on the scene for four days.

"Juba was just wonderful — just a very typical, high-energy, extremely intelligent dog," says Dyer of her wilderness, water, cadaver and urban disaster search dog who died just short of 10 years in June 1996. "The harder I worked her, the more she responded. Her drive and determination were just unbelievable.

"There will be many searches on cold, windy, rainy nights," she says. "I will be tired and wet. But if I start to get discouraged, all I have to do is look at my tireless Boxer who is willing to work cheerfully for as many hours as it takes. My spirit is lifted."

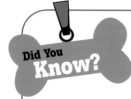
When Bang Away was in the ring, everyone went to watch him. His picture appeared not only in dog magazines but also in general interest magazines, such as *Life*, *Colliers* and *Esquire*. Airline pilots knew when he was on board, and he rode in the cabin, not in cargo. He eventually retired with 121 BIS wins. During his life, he sired more champions than any other Boxer and changed the look of the breed. Boxers became more streamlined, with a style and dash that had been previously lacking.

"An infatuation with flashy markings began after the war years with the arrival of Bang Away on the scene," says breeder Stephanie Abraham of Connecticut. "Then and now, many breeders selected their keepers based on which dogs had the most striking markings rather than the best conformation. In 1999, the American Boxer Club board of directors advised judges to give equal consideration to 'plain' Boxers, with the admonition that quality, not 'window dressing,' is paramount to the breed standard."

Since Bang Away, only one Boxer has taken BIS at Westminster. Her name was Ch. Arriba's Prima Donna, and she won in 1970. Her breeder, Ted Fickes, has produced more than 90 champions, many of which have become the foundation dogs for other Boxer breeding programs.

BOXERS IN THE 21ST CENTURY

According to today's breed standard, the ideal Boxer is a medium-sized, square-built dog of substance with a short back, strong limbs and short, tight-fitting coat. Beneath his taut skin, his well-developed muscles are clean and hard. His very being denotes energy as he covers ground with a smooth, ground-devouring stride and a proud carriage.

The Boxer's chiseled head with his upturned nose, square jaw and blunt muzzle is the breed's trademark and must show a harmonious proportion of muzzle to skull. The dog's mood-mirroring expression is unique, wrinkles typically appearing on the forehead when it is alert. The ears are cropped rather long and tapering when the breed is shown in the United States. Many pet owners now opt for the look of the uncropped, hanging natural ear the way the dog is shown in the United Kingdom.

The dog's broad chest, short back and sloping topline add to his proud bearing and squared-away appearance. His tail is docked short but still manages to happily

Just how quickly will your Boxer puppy grow? Go to Club Boxer and download a growth chart. You also can see your pup's age in human years. The old standard of multiplying your dog's age by seven isn't quite accurate. Log onto **DogChannel.com/Club-Boxer** and click on "Downloads."

JOIN OUR ONLINE **Club Boxer™**

Boxers are very intelligent but also very inquisitive. They want to know everything that is going on around them. Because of this, they can easily be distracted during obedience work. — Boxer breeder James Kilman of Grove City, Ohio

wag the dog. Compact in size, an adult male should stand 22 to 25 inches at the withers (shoulders); the female should measure 21 to 23 inches. Because there is no size disqualification, the emphasis is on proper balance and quality of the individual dog. The breed's ideal weight ranges from 53 to 71 pounds.

The only acceptable color in the standard is fawn, ranging from tan to mahogany, and the only acceptable combination is brindle, showing clearly defined stripes on a fawn body. White markings on the muzzle, chest, belly, feet, neck and inside legs are permissible but should not cover more than one-third of the dog's body. The face must have a black mask, but a white blaze is permitted from the muzzle upward between the eyes.

"Flash" refers to the amount of white on a dog and is considered acceptable and attractive, but an all-white Boxer is a controversy within the breed community. Such dogs cannot be shown, should not be bred and are not allowed to be registered with the AKC.

While it is difficult to separate fact from folklore on this topic, it is generally held that there is a high degree of deafness in white Boxers and that they also have a higher incidence of skin and eye problems. While the culling and euthanizing of white Boxers at birth is still practiced, many breeders opt to place them in loving homes either neutered or with a signed agreement that they will never be bred. Although barred from the conformation ring, white Boxers can compete in obedience and agility.

The Boxer is an athlete, requiring regular exercise to maintain that prized physique. While some breed enthusiasts recommend at least a mile walk each day, most agree that exercise within a fenced yard or frequent walking on a leash is adequate. Because they are inquisitive wanderers with a highly developed prey drive and often enjoy chasing bikes, cars or small animals, Boxers should never be allowed to run loose. A fenced yard makes life much easier for devoted enthusiasts.

Boxers meet with great success in the obedience ring. Their innate intelligence makes them quick learners, but they can sometimes have a mind of their own. They are also highly sensitive and should never be frightened or shamed. Positive reinforcement works best with these dogs whose owners insist they are almost human.

WORKING FOR A LIVING

A member of the AKC's Working Group, the Boxer has earned its stripes as a war dog, police dog, guardian, therapy dog and service dog. But within its role as a family companion this canine character really shines. With all the meticulous detail invested by its breeders in form and function, the most notable change in the breed in the last 100 years has been in its temperament, evolving from a vicious bull-fighter and war dog to a reserved and down-to-earth gentleman.

The desire for human affection is the Boxer's most notable characteristic. This remarkable dog is happiest as part of the family, especially if there are children to play with and protect. The Boxer seeks to please its humans, basking in the admiration it receives as it trots jauntily along by your side. Once you have owned a Boxer, it is hard to imagine living without this irreplaceable companion, truly a dog for all seasons.

THE BOXER

The decision is made. It has to be a Boxer. Your first step might be to attend dog shows to meet the people who love Boxers and to meet members of the breed face to face. A list of shows can be found in dog magazines or by calling a local breed club. Talk to the exhibitors; they are a fountain of information. Ask local kennel clubs or veterinarians for breeder referrals. People close to the breed know who the responsible breeders are and who has healthy animals.

But choosing a breeder involves more than finding one. Good breeders care deeply about their dogs; in fact, they care more about their dogs than making a sale. The bond of love between breeder and dogs may be invisible, but it is easy to see all the same: An almost unconscious caress of a velvety ear, an irresistible urge to touch their pet, a Boxer's adoring look when the breeder speaks, a welcoming wag that turns into a wiggle.

Look for other displays of affection for the breed, such as pictures, knickknacks or a T-shirt that boldly announces "Bonkers Over Boxers!" Breeders inundate themselves with reminders of their breed of choice.

EVALUATING BREEDERS

Once you have the names and numbers of breeders in your area, start contacting them to find out more about their breeding programs. But, before you pick up the phone, plan to ask the questions that will get you the information you need to know.

Prospective buyers interview breeders much the same way that a breeder should interview a buyer. Make a list of questions and record the answers so you can compare them to the answers from other breeders you may interview later. The right questions are those that help you identify who has been in the breed a respectable number of years and who is actively showing their dogs. Ask in-depth questions regarding the genetic health of the parents, grandparents and great grandparents of any puppy you are considering. Ask what sort of genetic testing program the breeder adheres to.

A prospective buyer should look to see if a breeder actively shows his or her Boxers. Showing indicates that the breeder is bringing out examples from his or her breeding program for the public to see. If there are any obvious problems, such as temperament or general conformation, they will be readily apparent. Also, the main reason to breed dogs is to improve the quality of the breed. If the breeder is not showing, then he or she is more likely to do it purely for the monetary aspect and may have less concern for the welfare and future of the breed.

Inquiring about health and determining the breeder's willingness to work with you in the future are also important duties for the potential puppy buyer. The prospective buyer should see what kind of health guarantees the breeder gives. You should also find out if the breeder will be available for

Don't fall for the first cute face you see in a litter. Ask the breeder for advice about which pup would best fit your life.

future consultation regarding your Boxer, and find out if the breeder will take your dog back if something unforeseen happens.

Prospective buyers should ask plenty of questions, and in return buyers should also be prepared to answer questions posed by a responsible breeder who wants to make sure his or her puppy is going to a good home. Be prepared for a battery of questions from the breeder regarding your purpose for wanting a Boxer and whether you can properly care for one. Avoid buying from a breeder who does little or no screening. If a breeder asks no questions, they are not concerned with where their pups end up. In this case, the dogs' best interests are probably not the breeder's motive for breeding.

The buyer should find a breeder who is willing to answer any questions they have and are knowledgeable about the breed's

Boxers are fun-loving, goofy clowns; bed hogs; face washers; shoe polishers; floor mops; better than blankets; the largest but ultimate lap dogs; and your best but most stubborn friends and soul mates. — breeder Sandy Orr of Omaha, Neb.

history, health issues and about the background of their own dogs. Learn about a breeder's long-term commitment to the breed and to his or her puppies after they leave the kennel.

Look for breeders who are knowledgeable in the pedigrees of their dogs and of the breed itself and have had the necessary health screenings performed on the parents. Good breeders should also ask you for references because they are interested in establishing a relationship with you. If after one phone conversation with a breeder, the person is supplying you with an address in which to send a deposit, continue your search for a reputable breeder elsewhere.

CHOOSING THE RIGHT PUP

Once you have found a breeder with whom you are comfortable, your next step is to pick the right puppy for you. The good news is that if you have done your homework in finding a responsible breeder, you can count on this person to give you plenty of help in choosing the right pup for your personality and lifestyle. In fact, most good breeders will recommend a specific puppy to a buyer once they know what kind of dog the buyer wants.

If the pup is being purchased as a show prospect, the breeder will offer his or her assessment of the pups that meet this criteria and be able to explain the strengths and faults of each pup.

Whether your new pup is show- or pet-quality, a good, stable temperament is vital for a happy relationship. Generally, you want to avoid a timid puppy or a very dominant one. Temperament is very important, and a reputable breeder should spend a lot of time with the pups and be able to offer an evaluation of each pup's personality.

Reputable breeders should tell you which puppy is appropriate for your home situation and personality. They may not allow you to choose the puppy, although they will certainly take your preference into consideration.

Chemistry between buyer and puppy is important and should play a role in determining which pup goes to which home. When possible, make numerous visits to see the puppies, and in effect, let a puppy choose you. There will usually be one puppy that spends more time with a buyer and is more comfortable relaxing and sitting with, or on, a person.

Most well-bred Boxer pups are social, rough-and-tumble little beings. Ask the breeder's opinion. Someone who's devoted the last eight weeks to these puppies wants them to be happy in the home that's right for them. Describe your lifestyle, your hopes and desires for the pup, and let the breeder guide you to the appropriate choice.

Have you thought about showing or competing in obedience and agility? If so, the litter owner likely will have some specific

---

Questions to Expect

Be prepared for the breeder to ask you questions, too. He's just looking for the best home for his pups.

1. Have you previously owned a Boxer?

The breeder is trying to gauge how familiar you are with the breed. If you have never owned one, illustrate your knowledge of Boxers by telling the breeder about your research.

2. Do you have children? What are their ages?

Some breeders are wary about sell-ing a dog to families with younger children. This isn't a steadfast rule, and some breeders only insist on meeting the children to see how they handle puppies. It all depends on the breeder.

3. How long have you wanted a Boxer?

This helps a breeder know if this purchase is an impulse buy or a carefully thought-out decision. Buying on impulse is one of the biggest mistakes owners can make. Be patient.

Join Club Boxer to get a complete list of questions a breeder should ask you. Click on "Downloads" at: **DogChannel.com/Club-Boxer**

requirements such as health testing or proving the dog's quality in the ring. Most people simply want a good companion dog, one that will be affectionate, playful and a valued member of the family. Responsible breeders — those who are aware of the overabundance of unwanted animals — will require new owners to spay or neuter their dog.

Be sure to ask breeders about the health and longevity of their lines. Sadly, the Boxer is not a long-lived breed. Life expectancy is 8 to 12 years, mainly because of cancers. Ask whether parents' hips have been certified "normal" by the Orthopedic Foundation for Animals. Stay away from lines that have rampant bloat, heart or cancer problems. Keep a close eye out for "Boxer bumps" or changes in weight, habits or physical well-being. Feed a high-quality, nutritious diet.

Ask to see the mother (also called the dam) of the litter. She is an excellent indication of how the pup will mature. Make allowances for saggy, baggy motherhood, but quality should still stand out. If you find the dam to be appealing and affectionate, her pup should be just as delightful when raised with proper guidance. In unusual circumstances such as a leased breeding or a trauma, the dam may be unavailable for viewing. In those cases, other relatives such as grandparents or siblings can also be an indication of temperament.

For those people who would like to show their Boxer, it's important to look for a breeder who has a track record for producing titles in the arena of your choice. The show pup should have sound movement, deep ribbing and slightly sloping

With the popularity of Boxers, shelters and rescue groups across the country are often inundated with sweet, loving examples of the breed — from the tiniest puppies to senior dogs, petite females to blocky males. Often, to get the Boxer of your dreams, it takes just a journey to the local shelter. Or perhaps you could find your ideal dog waiting patiently in the arms of a foster parent at a nearby rescue group. It just takes a bit of effort, patience and a willingness to find the right dog for your family, not just the cutest dog on the block.

The perks of owning a Boxer are plentiful: companionship, unconditional love, true loyalty and laughter, just to name a few. So why choose the adoption option? You are literally saving a life!

Owners of adopted dogs swear they're more grateful and loving than any dog they've owned before. It's almost as if they knew what dire fate awaited them and are so thankful to you. Boxers, known for their people-pleasing personalities, seem to embody this mentality wholeheartedly when they're rescued. And they want to give something back.

Another perk: Most adopted dogs come fully vetted, with proper medical treatment, vacci-nations, medicine, as well as being spayed or neutered. Some are even licensed and microchipped.

Don't disregard older dogs, thinking the only good pair-up is you and a puppy. Adult Boxers are more established behaviorally and personality-wise, helping to better mesh their characteristics with yours in this game of matchmaker. Puppies are always high in demand, so if you open your options to include adult dogs, you'll have a better chance of adopting quickly. Plus, adult dogs are often housetrained, more calm, chew-proof and don't need to be taken outside in the middle of the night ... five times ... in the pouring rain.

The American Boxer Club offers rescue information (www.americanboxerclub.org) or log onto Petfinder.com (www.petfinder.com). The site's searchable database enables you to find a Boxer puppy in your area who needs a break in the form of a compassionate owner like you. More websites are listed in the Resources chapter on page 166.

topline. His neck should be elegantly arched, and the body proportions should be square. A Boxer's head is one of the hallmarks of the breed and is highly important in choosing a winner.

If possible, bring a knowledgeable person along to view the litter. A breeder or dog show exhibitor — even one with another breed — often has a good eye for quality. Anyone who has a goal to finish a champion should be aware of the standard's requirements and, if not already a fancier, should find someone to aid them in their puppy selection.

The perfect owner for a Boxer is one who is active, sociable, outgoing and friendly, or a family with lots of children who can entertain their Boxer. The perfect owner is one who is willing to set boundaries and be a good, watchful puppy parent, or a family who enjoys spending time with its Boxer and including him in fun, outdoor activities. The perfect owner is a person who looks forward to arriving home and being greeted by a joyful and loyal companion dog, or people who plan to give their Boxer part of their home and heart.

CHECKING FOR BOXER QUALITIES

Whether you are dealing with a breeder who wants to pick a pup for you or lets you make the decision alone, consider certain points when evaluating the pup that you may end up calling your own. The pup should be friendly and outgoing, not skittish in any way. He should be forgiving of correction and shouldn't be too terribly mouthy. The pup should readily follow you and be willing to snuggle in your lap and be turned onto his back easily without a problem.

Proper temperament is important. A puppy who has a dominant personality requires an experienced owner who will be firm during training. A Boxer puppy who is a little shy requires heavy socialization to build his confidence.

Evaluate a puppy's temperament on your own, with the breeder's permission. The temperament can be evaluated by spending some time watching them. If you can visit the pups and observe them first together with their littermates, then you can see how they interact with each other. You may be able to pinpoint which ones are the bullies and which ones are more submissive. In

---

Breeder Q&A

Here are some questions you should ask a breeder and the answers you want.

Q. How often do you have litters available?

A. The answer you want to hear is "once or twice a year" because a breeder who doesn't have litters all that often is probably more concerned with the quality of his puppies, rather than making money.

Q. What kinds of health problems have you had with your Boxers?

A. Beware of a breeder who says "none." Every breed has health issues and a good breeder is aware of the illnesses that may run in his line. For Boxers, genetic health problems include cancer, dilated cardiomyopathy and others.

Get a complete list of questions to ask a Boxer breeder — and the correct answers — at Club Boxer. Log onto **DogChannel.com/Club-Boxer** and click on "Downloads."

general, look for a puppy that is more interested in you than his littermates. Then, take each pup individually to a new location away from the rest of the litter. Put the pup down on the ground, walk away and see how he reacts away from the security of his littermates. The pup may be afraid at first, but should gradually recover and start checking out his new surroundings

DO-IT-YOURSELF TEMPERAMENT TEST

Puppies come in a wide assortment of temperaments to suit just about everyone. If you are looking for a dog that is easily trainable and a general good companion to your family, you most likely want a dog with a medium temperament.

Temperament testing can help you determine the type of disposition your potential puppy possesses. A pup with a medium, trainable temperament will have the following reactions to these various tests, best conducted when the pup is 7 weeks old.

Step 1. To test a pup's social attraction to humans and his confidence or shyness in approaching them, coax your dog toward you by kneeling down and clapping your hands gently. A puppy with a medium temperament comes readily, tail up or tail down.

Step 2. To test a pup's eagerness to follow, walk away from him while he is watching you. The pup should follow you readily, tail up.

Step 3. To see how a Boxer puppy handles restraint, kneel down and roll the pup gently on his back. Using a light but firm touch, hold the Boxer in this position with one hand for 30 seconds. The pup should settle down after some initial struggle first and offer some or steady eye contact.

Step 4. To evaluate a pup's level of social dominance, stand up, then crouch down beside the pup and stroke him from head to back. A pup with a medium temperament, neither too dominant nor too submissive, should cuddle up to you and lick your face, or squirm and lick your hands.

Step 5. An additional test of a pup's dominance level is to bend over, cradle the pup under his belly with your fingers interlaced and palms up and elevate him just off the ground. Hold the puppy there for 30 seconds. The pup should not struggle and should be relaxed, or he should struggle and then settle down and lick you.

CHECK THAT PUPPY

To assess a puppy's health, take a deliberate, thorough look at each part of his body. A healthy puppy has bright eyes, a healthy coat, a good appetite and firm stool.

Watch for a telltale link between physical and mental health. A healthy Boxer, as with any breed of puppy, will display a happier, more positive attitude than an unhealthy puppy. A pup's belly should not be over extended or hard, as this may be a sign of worms. Also, if you are around the litter long enough to witness a bowel movement, the stool should be solid, and the pup should not show any signs of discomfort. Look into the pup's eyes, too. They should be bright and full of life.

When purchasing a puppy, buyers hear from breeders that Boxers are just like any other puppy — times 10! They are very smart, calculating, stubborn and often have their own agendas. If a prospective owner isn't willing to spend a fair amount of time with a Boxer, then the breed is not for them. A Boxer wants to be with people and is quite like a 7-year-old boy in that he needs attention and consistent reinforcement for behavioral parameters. Once through adolescence, however, this dog is the best friend and companion a person or family could have.

PUPPY PARTICULARS

Here are 10 things to look for when picking a puppy from a breeder. When in doubt, ask the breeder which puppy he or she thinks has the best personality and temperament to fit your lifestyle.

1. Look at the area where the pups spend most of their time. It's OK if they play outdoors part of the day, but they should sleep indoors at night so that the pups can interact with people and become accustomed to hearing ordinary household noises. This builds a solid foundation for a secure, well-socialized puppy. The puppy area should be clean, well lit, have fresh drinking water and interesting toys.

2. Sure, you're only buying one puppy, but make sure to see all of the puppies in the litter. By 5 weeks of age, healthy pups will begin playing with one another and should be lively and energetic. It's OK if they're asleep when you visit, but stay long enough to see them wake up. Once they're up, they shouldn't be lethargic or weak, as this may be a sign of illness.

3. Pups should be confident and eager to greet you. A pup who is shy or fearful and stays in the corner may be sick or insecure. Although some introverted

Boxer puppies learn fast and love to play. A smart owner will take the time to prepare for the new pup's homecoming.

pups come out of their shells later on, many do not. These dogs will always be fearful as adults and are not good choices for an active, noisy family with or without children, or for people who have never had a dog before. They are skittish and frighten easily, and will also require immense training and socialization in order to live a happy life.

Choose a pup who is happy and eager to interact with you; don't invest your time and attention in a puppy who is either too timid or too bossy. These temperament types are incredibly challenging and are difficult to manage. The perfect puppy personality is somewhere between these two extremes.

4. If it's feeding time during your visit, all pups should be eager to gobble up their food. Refusing to eat can be a sign of illness, so immediately have your Boxer checked by your vet.

5. The dog's skin should be smooth, clean and shiny without any sores or bumps. Puppies should not be biting or scratching at themselves continuously, which could signal fleas.

6. After 10 to 12 days, eyes should be open and clear without any redness or discharges. Pups should not be scratching at their eyes, as this may cause an infection or signal irritation.

7. Vomiting or coughing more than once is not normal. If this happens, the pup may be ill and should visit the veterinarian.

8. Visit long enough to see the pups eliminate. All stools should be firm without being watery or bloody. These are signs of illness or that a puppy has worms.

9. Boxer puppies should be able to walk around or run around freely without limping.

10. A healthy puppy who is getting enough to eat should not be skinny. You should be able to slightly feel his ribs if you rub his abdomen, but you should not be able to see the ribs protruding through the skin.

Signs of a Healthy Puppy

Here are a few things you should look for when selecting a puppy from a litter.

1. **NOSE:** It should be slightly moist to the touch but there shouldn't be excessive discharge. The puppy should not be sneezing or sniffling persistently.

2. **SKIN AND COAT:** Your Boxer puppy's coat should be soft and shiny, without flakes or excessive shedding. Watch out for patches of missing hair, redness, bumps or sores. The pup should have a pleasant smell. Check for parasites, such as fleas or ticks.

3. **BEHAVIOR:** A healthy Boxer puppy may be sleepy, but he should not be lethargic. A healthy pup will be playful at times, not isolated in a corner. You should see occasional bursts of energy and interaction with littermates. When it's mealtime, a healthy pup will take an interest in his food.

There are more things to look for when picking out the perfect Boxer puppy for you. Download the complete list at **DogChannel.com/Club-Boxer**

BREEDER PAPERS

Everything today comes with an instruction manual. When you purchase a Boxer, it's no different. A reputable breeder should give you a registration application; a sales contract; a health guarantee; the dog's complete health records; a three-, four- or five-generation pedigree; and some general information on behavior, care, conformation, health and training.

Registration Application. This document from the American Kennel Club or United Kennel Club assigns your puppy a number and identifies your dog by listing his date of birth, the names of the parents and shows that he is registered as a purebred Boxer. It does not prove whether or not your dog is a show- or a pet-quality Boxer and doesn't provide any health guarantee.

Sales Contract. A reputable breeder should discuss the terms of the contract before asking you to sign it. This is a written understanding of both of your expectations about the puppy and shows that the breeder cares about the puppy's welfare throughout his life. The contract can include such terms as requiring you to keep your dog indoors at night, spaying or neutering if the puppy is not going to be a show dog, providing routine veterinary care throughout your dog's life, and assurance that you'll feed your dog a healthy diet. Most responsible breeders will ask that you take your dog to obedience classes and earn a Canine Good Citizen (an AKC-sanctioned training program that promotes good manners in dogs) title before 2 years of age. Many breeders also require new owners to have totally secure fencing and gates around their yard.

Health Records. Here's everything you want to know about not only your puppy's health, but the parents' as well. It should include the dates the puppy was vaccinated, dewormed and examined by a veterinarian for signs of heart murmur, plus the parents' test results for the presence or absence of hip and elbow dysplasia, heart problems and luxated patellas.

Health Guarantee. This includes a letter from a veterinarian that the puppy has been examined and is healthy, and states that the breeder will replace your dog if the pup develops a genetic, life-threatening illness during his lifetime.

Pedigree. Breeders should give you a copy of the puppy's three-, four- or five-generation pedigree. Many breeders also have photos of your dog's ancestors they will proudly share with you.

Information. The best breeders pride themselves on handing over a notebook full of the latest information on Boxer behavior, care, conformation, health and training. Be sure to read it because it will provide valuable help while raising your dog.

Don't for one second think that a Boxer would prefer to live in a place described as a ring or a gym! He, like every other breed, wants to live in the best accommodations with plenty of toys, soft bedding and other luxuries. Your home is now his home, too. And before you even bring that new puppy or rescue dog into his new forever home, you need to make it accessible for him.

In fact, in order for him to grow into a stable, well-adjusted dog, he has to feel comfortable in his surroundings. Remember, he is leaving the warmth and security of his mother and littermates, as well as the familiarity of the only place he has ever known, so it is important to make his transition to your home — his new home — as easy as possible.

PUPPY-PROOFING

Aside from making sure that your Boxer will be comfortable in your home, you also have to ensure that your home is safe, which means taking the proper precautions to keep your pup away from things that are dangerous for him.

it's a Fact

Dangers lurk indoors and outdoors. Keep your curious Boxer from investigating your shed and garage. Antifreeze and fertilizers, such as those you would use for roses, will kill a Boxer. Keep these items on high shelves that are out of reach of your dog.

A smart owner will create a safe outdoor environment for their Boxer to explore and enjoy.

Puppy-proof your home inside and outside before bringing your Boxer home for the first time. Place breakables out of reach. If he is limited to certain places within the house, keep potentially dangerous items in off-limit areas. If your Boxer is going to spend time in a crate, make sure that there is nothing near it that he can reach if he sticks his curious nose or paws through the openings.

The outside of your home must also be safe. Your pup will want to run and explore the yard, and he should be granted that freedom — as long as you are there to supervise him. Do not let a fence give you a false sense of security; you would be surprised how crafty (and persistent) a Boxer can be in figuring out how to dig under a fence or squeeze his way through holes. The solution is to make the fence well embedded into the ground. Be sure to repair or secure any gaps in the fence. Check the fence periodically to ensure that it is in good shape and make repairs as needed; a very determined Boxer pup may work on the same spot until he is able to get through.

The following are a few common problem areas to watch out for in the home.

■ **Electrical cords and wiring:** No electrical cord or wiring is safe. Many office-supply stores sell products to keep wires gathered under desks, as well as products that prevent office chair wheels (and puppy teeth) from damaging electrical cords. If you have exposed cords and wires, these products aren't very expensive and can be used to keep a Boxer pup out of trouble.

■ **Trash cans:** Don't waste your time trying to train your Boxer not to get into the trash. Simply put the garbage behind a cabinet door and use a child-proof lock if necessary. Dogs love bathroom trash (e.g., cotton balls and cotton swabs, used razors, dental floss), which are all extremely dangerous! Be proactive and place the trash can in a cabinet under the sink and make sure to always shut the bathroom door.

■ **Household cleaners:** Make sure your Boxer doesn't have access to any of these deadly chemicals. Keep them behind closed cabinet doors — using child-proof locks if necessary — or on high shelves.

■ **Pest control sprays and poisons:** Chemicals to control ants or other pests should never be used in the house, if possible. Your pup doesn't have to directly ingest these poisons to become ill; if your

A well-stocked toy box should contain three main categories of toys.
1. **action** — anything that you can throw or roll and get things moving
2. **distraction** — durable toys that make dogs work for a treat
3. **comfort** — soft, stuffed little "security blankets"

Boxer steps in the poison, he can contract the toxic effects simply by licking his paws. Roach motels and other poisonous pest traps are also appealing to dogs, so don't place these behind couches or cabinets; if there's room for a roach motel, there's room for a curious and determined Boxer.

■ **Fabric:** Here's one you might not think about: Some puppies have a habit of licking blankets, upholstery, rugs or carpets. Though this habit seems fairly innocuous, over time the fibers from the upholstery or carpet can accumulate in your dog's stomach and create a blockage. If you see your dog licking these items, immediately remove the item or prevent him from having contact with it.

■ **Prescriptions, painkillers, supplements and vitamins:** Keep all medications stored in a cabinet. Be very careful when taking your prescription medications, supplements or vitamins. How often have you dropped a pill? With a Boxer, you can be sure that your puppy will be at your feet and will snarf up the pill before you can even start to say "No!" Dispense your pills carefully and without your Boxer present.

■ **Miscellaneous loose items:** If it's not bolted to the floor, your puppy is likely to give the item a taste test. Socks, coins, children's toys, game pieces, cat bell balls

— you name it. If it's on the floor, it's worth a try. Make sure the floors in your home are picked up and free of clutter.

FAMILY INTRODUCTIONS

Everyone in the house will be excited about the puppy's homecoming and will want to pet and play with him, but it is best to make the introduction low-key so as not to overwhelm the puppy. He already will be apprehensive. It is the first time he has been separated from his mother, littermates and the breeder, and the ride to your home is likely to be the first time he has been in a car. The last thing you want to do is smother your Boxer, as this will only frighten him further. This is not to say that human contact is not extremely necessary at this stage because this is the time when a connection between the pup and his human family is formed. Gentle petting and soothing words should help console your Boxer, as well as just putting him down and letting him explore on his own (under your watchful eye, of course).

The first thing you should always do before your puppy comes home is to lie on the ground and look around. You want to be able to see everything your puppy is going to see. For the puppy, the world is one big chew toy.

— Cathleen Stamm, rescue volunteer in San Diego, Calif.

Your pup may approach the family members or may busy himself with exploring for a while. Gradually, each person should spend some time with the pup, one at a time, crouching down to get as close to the Boxer's level as possible and letting him sniff their hands before petting him gently. He definitely needs human attention and he needs to be touched; this is how to form an immediate bond. Just remember that the pup is experiencing a lot of things for the first time, at the same time. There are new people, new noises, new smells and new things to investigate, so be gentle, be affectionate and be as comforting as you can be.

SMART TIP!

9-1-1! If you don't know whether the plant or food or "stuff" your Boxer just ate is toxic to dogs, you can call the ASPCA's Animal Poison Control Center (888-426-4435). Be prepared to provide your puppy's age and weight, her symptoms and how much of the substance she ingested, as well as how long ago you think she came into contact with the substance. The ASPCA charges a consultation fee for this service.

A smart owner will check indoor and outdoor plants to make sure they aren't poisonous or dangerous to a Boxer.

Everyone who rides in your car has to buckle up — even your Boxer! Your dog can travel in the car inside her crate or you can use a doggie seat belt. These look like harnesses that attach to your car's seat-belt system.

PUP'S FIRST NIGHT HOME

You have traveled home with your new charge safely in his crate. He may have already been to the vet for a thorough check-up; he's been weighed, his papers examined, perhaps he's even been vaccinated and wormed as well. Your Boxer has met and licked the whole family, including the excited children and the less-than-

happy cat. He's explored his area, his new bed, the yard and anywhere else he's permitted. He's eaten his first meal at home and relieved himself in the proper place. Your Boxer has heard lots of new sounds, smelled new friends and seen more of the outside world than ever before.

This was just the first day! He's worn out and is ready for bed — or so you think! Remember, this is your puppy's first night to sleep alone. His mother and littermates are no longer at paw's length, and he's scared, cold and lonely. Be reassuring to your new family member. This is not the time to spoil your Boxer and give in to his inevitable whining.

Puppies whine. They whine to let others know where they are and hopefully to get company out of it. Place your Boxer puppy in his new bed or crate in his room and close the door. Mercifully, he may fall

Boxers adjust well to new homes. Get ready for all the good times to come!

Playing with toys from puppyhood encourages good behavior and social skills throughout your dog's life. A happy, playful dog is a content and well-adjusted one. Also, because all puppies chew to soothe their gums and help loosen puppy teeth, dogs should always have easy access to several different toys.

— dog trainer and author Harrison Forbes from Savannah, Tenn.

SMART TIP!

Keep a crate in your vehicle and take your Boxer along when you visit the drive-through at the bank or your favorite fast-food restaurant. She can watch interactions, hear interesting sounds and maybe garner a dog treat.

his former home in his new bed so that he recognizes the scent of his littermates. Others advise placing a hot water bottle in his bed for warmth. The latter may be a good idea provided the pup doesn't attempt to suckle; he'll get good and wet and may not fall asleep so fast.

Your Boxer's first night can be somewhat terrifying for him and his new family. Remember that you set the tone of nighttime at your house. Unless you want to play with your pup every night at 10 p.m., midnight and 2 a.m., don't initiate the habit. Your family will thank you and so will your pup!

asleep without a peep. If the inevitable occurs, ignore the whining; he is fine. Do not give in and visit your Boxer puppy. He will fall asleep eventually. Many breeders recommend placing a piece of bedding from

Toys are a great way for your Boxer to experience the world. A smart owner will check toys regularly to ensure their safety.

SHOPPING FOR A BOXER

It's fun shopping for a new puppy. From training to feeding and sleeping to playing, your new Boxer will need a few items to make life comfy, easy and fun. Be prepared and visit your local pet-supply store before you bring home your new family member.

◆ **Collar and ID tag:** Accustom your dog to wearing a collar the first day you bring him home. Not only will a collar and ID tag help your pup in the event that he becomes lost, but collars are also an important training tool. If your Boxer gets into trouble, the collar will act as a handle, helping you

Funny Bone

To err is human; to forgive, canine.

— *Anonymous*

divert him to a more appropriate behavior. Make sure the collar fits snugly enough so that your Boxer cannot wriggle out of it, but is loose enough so that it will not be uncomfortably tight around his neck. You should be able to fit a finger between the pup and the collar. Collars come in many styles, but for starting out, a simple buckle collar with an easy-release snap works great. Harnesses work well, too.

◆ **Leash:** For training or just for taking a stroll down the street, a leash is your Boxer's vehicle to explore the outside world. Like collars, leashes come in a variety of styles and materials. A 6-foot nylon leash is a popular choice because it is lightweight and durable. As your pup grows and gets used to walking on the leash, you may want to purchase a flexible leash. These leads allow you to extend the length to give the dog a broader area to explore or to shorten the length to keep the dog closer to you.

◆ **Bowls:** Your dog will need two bowls — one for water and one for food. You may want two sets of bowls, one for inside and one for outside, depending on where

A new toy is very entertaining, but nothing can substitute playing one-on-one with your Boxer.

When you are unable to watch your Boxer puppy, put her in a crate or an exercise pen on an easily cleanable floor. If she does have an accident on carpeting, clean it completely and meticulously so it won't smell like her potty.

your dog will be fed and where he will be spending time. Bowls should be sturdy so that they don't tip over easily. Most have reinforced bottoms that prevent tipping. Bowls are usually made of metal, ceramic or plastic, and they should be easy to clean.

◆ **Crate:** A multipurpose crate serves as a bed, housetraining tool and travel carrier. It also is the ideal doggie den — a bedroom of sorts — that your Boxer can retire to when he wants to rest or just needs a break. The crate should be large enough for your Boxer to stand, turn around and lie down. You don't want any more room than this — especially if you're planning on using the crate to house-train your dog — because he will eliminate in one corner and lie down in another. Get a crate that is big enough for your dog when he is an adult; use dividers to limit the space when he's a puppy.

◆ **Bed:** A plush doggie bed will make sleeping and resting more comfortable for your Boxer. Dog beds come in all shapes, sizes and colors, but your dog just needs one that is soft and large enough for him to stretch out on. Because puppies and rescue dogs often don't come housetrained, it's helpful to buy a bed that can be easily washed. If your Boxer will be sleeping in a crate, a nice crate pad and a small blanket that he can burrow in will help him feel more at home. Replace the blanket if it becomes ragged and starts to fall apart because your Boxer's nails

could get caught in it.

◆ **Gate:** Similar to those used for toddlers, gates help keep your Boxer confined to one room or area when you can't supervise him. Gates also work to keep your dog out of areas you don't want him in. Boxers need strong gates to restrict them, otherwise they can tear through the gates with their muscular bodies.

◆ **Toys:** Keep your dog occupied and entertained by providing him with an array of fun toys. Teething puppies like to chew — in fact, chewing is a physical need for pups as they are teething — and everything from your shoes to the leather couch to the rug are fair game. Divert your Boxer's chewing instincts with durable toys like bones made of nylon or hard rubber.

Other fun toys include rope toys, treat-dispensing toys and balls. Make sure the toys and bones don't have small parts that could break off and be swallowed, causing your dog to choke. Stuffed toys can become de-stuffed, and an overexcited puppy may ingest the stuffing or squeaker. Check your Boxer's toys regularly and replace them if they become frayed or show signs of wear.

◆ **Cleaning supplies:** Until your pup is housetrained, you will be doing a lot of cleaning. Accidents will occur, which is acceptable in the beginning because the puppy doesn't know any better. All you can do is be prepared to clean up any accidents. Old rags, towels, newspapers and a stain-and-odor remover are good to have around the house.

BEYOND THE BASICS

The items previously discussed are the bare necessities. You will find out what else you need as you go along — grooming supplies, flea/tick protection, etc. These things will vary depending on your situation but it is important that you have everything you need to make your Boxer comfortable in his

Some ordinary household items make great toys for your Boxer — as long as they are safe. You will find a list of homemade toys at **DogChannel.com/Club-Boxer** — just click "Downloads."

HOUSETRAINING

Unexciting as it may be, the house-training part of puppy rearing greatly affects the budding relationship between a smart owner and his puppy — particularly when it becomes an area of ongoing contention. Fortunately, armed with suitable knowledge, patience and common sense, you'll find housetraining progresses at a relatively smooth rate. That leaves more time for the important things, like cuddling your adorable puppy, showing him off and laughing at his numerous antics.

The answer to successful housetraining is total supervision and management — crates, tethers, exercise pens and leashes — until you know your Boxer puppy has developed substrate preferences for outside surfaces (grass, gravel, concrete) instead of carpet, tile or hardwood, and he knows that potty happens outside.

IN THE BEGINNING

For the first two to three weeks of a puppy's life, his mother helps him eliminate. The mother also keeps the whelping box, or "nest area," clean. When pups begin to walk around and eat on their own, they choose where they eliminate. You can train your

it's a Fact

Ongoing housetraining difficulties may indicate your puppy has a health problem, warranting a veterinary checkup. A urinary infection, parasites, a virus and other nasty issues greatly affect your puppy's ability to hold it.

A smart owner will keep a vigilant eye on a puppy who is being housetrained. Remember to always use positive reinforcement!

puppy to relieve himself wherever you choose, but this must be somewhere suitable. You should bear in mind from the outset that when your puppy is old enough to go out in public places, any canine deposits must be removed at once. You will always have to carry a small plastic bag or poop-scoop with you.

Did You Know? Cleaning accidents properly with an enzyme solution will dramatically reduce the time it takes to house-train your dog because she won't be drawn back to the same areas.

Outdoor training includes such surfaces as grass, soil and concrete. Indoor training usually means training your dog on newspaper. When deciding on the surface and location that you will want your Boxer to use, be sure it is going to be permanent. Training your dog on grass and then changing two months later is difficult for both dog and owner.

Next, choose the cue you will use each time you want your puppy to void. "Let's go," "hurry up" and "potty" are examples of cues commonly used by smart Boxer owners.

Get in the habit of giving your puppy the chosen relief cue before you take him out. That way, when he becomes an adult, you will be able to determine if he wants to go out when you ask him. A confirmation will be signs of interest, such as wagging his tail, watching you intently, going to the door, etc.

LET'S START WITH THE CRATE

Clean animals by nature, dogs keenly dislike soiling where they sleep and eat. This fact makes a crate a useful housetraining tool. When purchasing a new crate, the correct size will allow adequate room for an adult Boxer to stand full height, lie on his side without scrunching and turn around easily. If debating plastic versus wire crates, short-haired breeds sometimes prefer the warmer, draft-blocking quality of plastic, while furry dogs often like the cooling airflow of a wire crate.

Some crates come equipped with a movable wall that reduces the interior size to provide enough space for your puppy to stand, turn and lie down, while not allowing room to soil one end and sleep in the other. The problem is if your puppy goes potty in the crate anyway, the divider forces him to lie in his own excrement.

This can work against you because it will desensitize your puppy against his normal instinctive revulsion to resting where he's eliminated. If scheduling permits you or a responsible family member to clean the crate soon after it's soiled, then you can continue to cratetrain because limiting crate size does encourage your puppy to hold it. Otherwise, give him enough room to move away from an unclean area until he's better able to control his elimination.

Needless to say, not every puppy adheres to this guideline. If your puppy moves along at a faster pace, thank your lucky stars. Should he progress slower, accept this and remind yourself that he'll improve. Be aware that pups frequently hold it longer at night than during the day. Just because your puppy sleeps for six or more hours through the night, it does not mean he can hold it that long during more active daytime hours.

One last bit of advice on the crate: Place it in the corner of a normally trafficked room, such as the family room or kitchen. Social and curious by nature, dogs like to feel included in family happenings. Creating a quiet retreat by putting the crate in an unused area may seem like a good idea, but it results in your puppy feeling insecure and isolated. Watching his people pop in and out of the crate-room will reassure your puppy that he's not forgotten.

Housetraining is key to your happiness, as well as your Boxer's.

PUPPY'S NEEDS

Your puppy needs to relieve himself after play periods, after each meal, after he has been sleeping and any time he indicates he is looking for a place to urinate or defecate.

The urinary and intestinal tract muscles of very young puppies are not fully developed. Therefore, like babies, puppies need to relieve themselves frequently. Take your Boxer puppy out often — every hour for an 8-week-old, for example — and immediately after sleeping and eating. The older the puppy, the less often he will need to relieve himself. Finally, as a healthy adult, he will require only three to five relief trips every day.

HOUSING HELPS

Because the types of housing and control you provide for your Boxer puppy have a direct relationship with housetraining success, you must consider the various aspects of both before beginning training. Taking a new puppy home and turning him loose in your house can be compared to turning a

child loose in a sports arena and telling the child that the place is all his! The sheer enormity of the place would be too much for him to handle. Instead, offer your puppy clearly defined areas where he can play, sleep, eat and live. A room of the house where the family gathers is the most obvious choice.

Dogs are social animals and need to feel like they are a part of the pack right from the start. Hearing your voice, watching you while you are doing things and smelling you nearby are all positive reinforcers that he is now a member of your pack. Usually a family room, the kitchen or a nearby adjoining breakfast area is ideal for providing safety and security for puppy and owner.

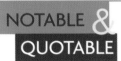

NOTABLE & QUOTABLE

Reward your pup with a high-value treat immediately after she potties to reinforce going in the proper location, then play for a short time afterward. This teaches that good things happen after pottying outside! — Victoria Schade, certified dog trainer, from Annandale, Va.

SMART TIP!

If you acquire your puppy at 8 weeks of age, expect to take her out at least six to eight times a day. By the time she's about 6 months old, potty trips will be down to three or four times a day. A rule of thumb is to take your puppy out in hourly intervals equal to her age in months.

Be consistent with when and where you take your puppy to potty. It'll make training much easier.

Within that room, there should be a smaller area that your Boxer puppy can call his own. An alcove, a wire or fiberglass dog crate or a fenced (not boarded!) corner from which he can view the activities of his new family will be fine. The size of the area or crate is key. The area must be large enough for the puppy to lie down and stretch out his body, yet small enough so he cannot relieve himself at one end and sleep at the other without coming into contact with his droppings before he is fully trained to relieve himself elsewhere.

Dogs are, by nature, clean animals and will not remain close to their relief areas unless forced to do so. In those cases, they then become dirty dogs and usually remain that way for life.

The designated area should be lined with clean bedding and a toy. Water must always be available in a nonspill container, once the dog is reliably housetrained.

IN CONTROL

By control, we mean helping your puppy create a lifestyle pattern that will be compatible to that of his human pack (you!). Just as we guide children to learn our way of life, we must show our pup when it is time to play, eat, sleep, exercise and entertain himself.

Your Boxer puppy should always sleep in his crate. He should also learn that, during times of household confusion and excessive human activity, such as at breakfast when family members are preparing for the day, he can play by himself in relative safety and comfort in his designated area. Each time you leave your Boxer alone, he should understand exactly where he is to stay.

Puppies are chewers. They cannot tell the difference between lamp cords, television

wires, shoes or table legs. Chewing into a television wire, for example, can be fatal to the puppy, and a shorted wire can start a fire in the house.

If the puppy chews on the arm of the chair when he is alone, you probably will discipline him angrily when you get home. Thus, he makes the association that your

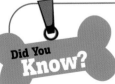

Did You Know? White vinegar is a good odor remover if you don't have any professional cleaners on hand; use one-quarter cup to one quart of water.

SMART TIP!

When proximity prevents you from going home at lunch or during periods when overtime crops up, make alternative arrangements for getting your pup outside. Hire a pet-sitting or walking service, or enlist the aid of a good neighbor.

coming home means he is going to be punished. He will not remember chewing the chair and is incapable of making the association of the discipline with his naughty deed.

Other times of excitement, such as family parties, can be fun for your puppy, provided that he can view the activities from the security of his designated area. This way he is not underfoot and is not being fed all sorts of tidbits that will probably cause him stomach distress, yet he still feels a part of the action.

SCHEDULE A SOLUTION

A Boxer puppy should be taken to his relief area each time he is released from his designated area, after meals, after play sessions and when he first awakens in the morning (at age 8 weeks, this can mean 5 a.m.!). The puppy will indicate that he's ready "to go" by circling or sniffing busily; do not misinterpret these signs. For a Boxer puppy less than 10 weeks of age, a routine of taking him out every hour might be necessary. As the puppy grows, he will be able to wait for longer periods of time.

Keep trips to your puppy's relief area short. Stay no more than five or six minutes, and then return to the house. If he goes during that time, praise him lavishly and take him indoors immediately. If he doesn't, but has an accident when you go back indoors, pick him up immediately, say "No!" and return to his relief area. Wait a few minutes, then return to the house again. Never hit your puppy or rub his face in urine or excrement when he has had an accident.

Once indoors, put your puppy in his crate until you have had time to clean up his accident. Then release him to the family area and watch him more closely than before. Chances are, his accident was a result of your not picking up his potty signals or waiting too long before offering him the opportunity to relieve himself. Never hold a grudge against your puppy for accidents.

Let the puppy learn that going outdoors means it is time to relieve himself, not to play. Once trained, he will be able to play indoors and out and still differentiate between the times for play versus the times for relief.

Help him develop regular hours for naps, being alone, playing by himself and just

10 HOUSETRAINING HOW-TOS

1. Decide where you want your Boxer to eliminate. Take her there every time until she gets the idea. Pick a spot that's easy to access. Remember, puppies have very little time between "gotta go" and "oops."

2. Teach an elimination cue, such as "go potty" or "get busy." Say this every time you take your Boxer to eliminate. Don't keep chanting the cue, just say it once or twice then keep quiet so you won't distract her.

3. Praise calmly when your dog eliminates, but stand there a little longer in case there's more.

4. Keep potty outings for potty only. Take the dog to the designated spot, tell her "go potty" and just stand there. If she needs to eliminate, she will do so within five minutes.

5. Don't punish for potty accidents; punishment can hinder progress. If you catch your Boxer in the act indoors, verbally interrupt but don't scold. Gently carry or lead your pup to the approved spot, let her finish, then praise.

6. If it's too late to interrupt an accident, scoop the poop or blot up the urine afterward with a paper towel. Immediately take your Boxer and her deposit (gently!) to the potty area. Place the poop or trace of urine on the ground and praise the pup. If she sniffs at its waste, praise more. Let your Boxer know you're pleased when her waste is in the proper area.

7. Keep track of when and where your Boxer eliminates — that will help you anticipate potty times. Regular meals mean regular elimination, so feed your dog scheduled, measured meals instead of free-feeding (leaving food available at all times).

8. Hang a bell on a sturdy cord from the doorknob. Before you open the door to take your Boxer out for potty, shake the string and ring the bell. Most dogs soon realize the connection between the bell ringing and the door opening, then they'll try it out for themselves. So, listen for that bell!

9. Dogs naturally return to re-soil where they've previously eliminated, so thoroughly clean up all accidents. Household cleaners usually will do the job, but special enzyme solutions may work better.

10. If the ground is littered with too much waste, your Boxer may seek a cleaner place to eliminate. Scoop the potty area daily, leaving just a single "reminder."

resting, all in his crate. Encourage him to entertain himself while you are busy elsewhere. Let him learn that having you nearby is comforting, but it is not your main purpose in life to provide him with undivided attention.

Each time you put or ask your Boxer puppy to go to his own area, use the same cue, whatever suits you best. Soon he will run to his crate or special area when he hears you say those words.

Remember that one of the primary ingredients in housetraining your puppy is control. Regardless of your lifestyle, there will always be occasions when you will need to have a place where your dog can stay and be happy and safe. Cratetraining is the answer for now and in the future.

Consistency, frequency, praise, control and supervision are all you really need to successfully housetrain your Boxer. By following these procedures you and your dog will soon be past the stage of accidents and ready to move on to a full and rewarding life together.

Having housetraining problems with your Boxer? Ask other Boxer owners for advice and tips. Log onto **DogChannel.com/Club-Boxer** and click on "Community."

EVERYDAY CARE

Your selection of a veterinarian should be based on personal recommendation for the doctor's skills with dogs, and if possible, Boxers. If the vet is based nearby, it will be helpful because you might have an emergency or need to make multiple visits for treatments.

FIRST STEP: SELECT THE RIGHT VET

All licensed veterinarians are capable of dealing with routine medical issues such as infections and injuries, as well as the promotion of health (for example, with vaccinations). If the problem affecting your Boxer is more complex, your vet will refer you to someone with more detailed knowledge of what is wrong. This usually will be a specialist like a veterinary dermatologist, veterinary ophthalmologist, etc. — whatever field you require.

Veterinary procedures are very costly, and as the treatments improve, they are going to become more expensive. It is quite acceptable to discuss matters of cost with your vet; if there is more than one treatment option, cost may be a factor in deciding which route to take.

Smart owners will look for a veterinarian before they actually need one. Newbie dog owners should start looking for a veterinarian a month or two before they bring home a new Boxer puppy. That will afford time to meet veterinarians, check out the condition of the clinic, meet the staff and see who they feel most comfortable with. If you already have a Boxer puppy, look sooner rather than later, preferably not in the midst of a veterinary health crisis.

Second, define the criteria that are important to you. Points to consider or investigate:

Convenience: Proximity to your home, extended hours or drop-off services are helpful for people who work regular business hours, have a busy schedule or don't want to drive far. If you have mobility issues, finding a vet who makes house calls or a service that provides pet transport might be particularly important.

Size: A one-person practice ensures that you will always be dealing with the same vet during each and every visit. "That person can really get to know you and your dog," says Bernadine Cruz, D.V.M., of Laguna Hills Animal Hospital in Laguna Hills, Calif. The downside, however, is that the sole practitioner does not have the immediate input of another vet, and, if your vet becomes ill or takes time off, there isn't anyone available to check your Boxer.

The multiple-doctor practice offers convenience if your Boxer unexpectedly needs medical treatment on a day when your veterinarian isn't there. Additionally, your vet can quickly consult with his colleagues within the clinic if he's unsure about a diagnosis or a treatment.

If you find a veterinarian within that practice who you really like, you can make your appointments with that individual, establishing the same kind of bond that you would with the solo practitioner.

Appointment Policies: Some veterinarian practices are strictly by-appointment only, which could minimize your wait time. However, if a sudden problem arises with your Boxer and the vets are booked up, they might not be able to squeeze your pet in that day. Some clinics are drop-in only — great for impromptu or crisis visits, but without scheduling may involve longer waits to see the next available veterinarian — whoever is open, not anyone in particular. Some practices maintain an appointment schedule but also keep slots open throughout the day for walk-ins, offering the best of both worlds.

Basic vs. State-of-the-Art vs. Full Service: A practice with high-tech equipment offers greater diagnostic capabilities and treatment options, important for tricky or difficult cases. However, the cost of pricey equipment is passed along to the client, so you could pay more for routine procedures. Some practices offer boarding, grooming, training classes and other services on the premises, which Boxer owners appreciate.

Fees and Payment Polices: How much is a routine office call? If there is a significant price difference, ask why. If you intend to carry health insurance on your Boxer or want to pay by credit card, make sure the candidate clinic accepts those payment options.

FIRST VET VISIT

It is much easier, less costly and more effective to practice preventive medicine than to fight bouts of illness and disease. Properly bred puppies of all breeds should

Did You Know?

Obesity is linked to the earlier onset of age-related health problems. Keep weight in line by providing your Boxer with sufficient exercise and play and by feeding proper serving sizes. Caloric requirements decline as your puppy reaches adulthood and can drop 25 to 30 percent within a couple of months after spaying/neutering. You'll probably need to reduce serving portions and switch to a less calorie-dense diet.

come from parents who were selected based upon their genetic disease profile. The puppies' mother should have been vaccinated, free of all internal and external parasites, and properly nourished. For these reasons, a visit to the veterinarian who cared for the dam (mother) is recommended if at all possible. The dam passes disease resistance to her puppies, which should last from 8 to 10 weeks. Unfortunately, she can also pass on parasites and infection. This is why knowledge about her health is useful in learning more about the health of her puppies.

Now that you have your Boxer puppy home safe and sound, it's time to arrange your pup's first trip to the veterinarian. Perhaps the breeder can recommend someone in the area who specializes in Boxers, or maybe you know other Boxer owners who can suggest a good vet. Either way, you should make an appointment within a couple of days of bringing your puppy home. If possible, see if you can stop for this first vet appointment before going home.

The pup's first vet visit will consist of an overall examination to make sure the pup does not have any problems that are not apparent to you. The veterinarian will also set up a schedule for the pup's vaccinations; the breeder will inform you of which ones the dog has already received and the vet can continue from there.

Your puppy also will have his teeth examined and have his skeletal conformation and general health checked prior to certification by the veterinarian. Pups in certain breeds have problems with their kneecaps, cataracts and other eye problems, heart murmurs and undescended testicles. They may also have personality problems, so ask your veterinarian if he or she has training in temperament evaluation.

VACCINATION SCHEDULING

Most vaccinations are given by injection and should only be given by a veterinarian. Both you and your vet should keep a record of the date of the injection, the identification of the vaccine and the amount given. Some vets give a first vaccination at 8 weeks of age, but most dog breeders prefer the course not to commence until about 10 weeks because of interaction with the antibodies produced by the mother. The vaccination scheduling is usually based on a 15-day cycle. You must take your vet's advice as to when to vaccinate, as this may differ according to the vaccine used.

The usual vaccines contain immunizing doses of several different viruses such as distemper, parvovirus, parainfluenza and hepatitis. There are other vaccines available when the puppy is at risk; rely on your vet's advice. This is especially true for the booster immunizations, most vaccination programs require a booster when the puppy is a year old and once a year thereafter. In some cases, circumstances may require more frequent immunizations.

Kennel cough, more formally known as *tracheobronchitis*, is immunized against with a vaccine sprayed into your dog's nostrils. Kennel cough is usually included in routine vaccinations, but it is often not as effective as the vaccines for other major diseases.

Your veterinarian will probably recommend your Boxer puppy be fully vaccinated before you take him on outings. There are airborne diseases, parasite eggs in the grass and unexpected visits from other dogs that might be dangerous to your puppy's health. Other dogs are the most harmful source of pathogenic organisms, as everything they have can be transmitted to your puppy.

6 Months to 1 Year of Age: Unless you intend to breed or show your dog, neutering

Set up a vet visit before you bring your new dog home, so you can interview the veterinarian staff.

Boxers are high-energy dogs. They can be destructive if not given structure, training, exercise and good management within the home. I suggest that owners find good, healthy outlets for their Boxers by providing them with structured exercise such as retrieving a ball or flying disc, swimming or getting involved in sports such as agility or flyball.

— dog trainer Kim Toepfer from Fresno, Calif.

The best part of being a new Boxer puppy owner is that you get to shower your little guy with love and affection.

or spaying your puppy at 6 months of age is recommended. Discuss this with your veterinarian. Neutering/spaying has proven to be beneficial to male and female puppies, respectively. Besides eliminating the possibility of pregnancy, it inhibits (but does not prevent) breast cancer in females and prostate cancer in male dogs.

Your veterinarian should perform a thorough dental evaluation on your Boxer puppy at 6 months, ascertaining whether all his permanent teeth have erupted properly. A home dental care regimen should be initiated at 6 months, including weekly brushing and providing good dental devices (such as nylon bones). Regular dental care promotes healthy teeth, fresh breath and a longer life.

Dogs Older Than 1 Year: Continue to visit the veterinarian at least once a year. There is no such disease as "old age," but

NOTABLE & QUOTABLE

It is our responsibility as breeders to support the researchers who have shown an interest in the diseases that affect our breed. Not only must we raise money to offer them financial support, we must participate in the studies with our dogs and be willing to share our test results, pedigrees and information.

— *Wendy A. Wallner, D.V.M. and Boxer breeder from Loganville, Ga.*

When selecting a veterinarian, make sure he or she is familiar with Boxers.

bodily functions do change with age. The eyes and ears are no longer as efficient As they once were. Liver, kidney and intestinal functions often decline. Proper dietary changes, recommended by your veterinarian, can make life more pleasant for you and your aging Boxer.

EVERYDAY HAPPENINGS

Keeping your Boxer healthy is a matter of keen observation and quick action when necessary. Knowing what's normal for your dog will help you recognize signs of trouble

before they blossom into a full-blown emergency situation.

Even if the problem is minor, such as a cut or scrape, you'll want to care for it immediately to prevent infection, as well as to ensure that your dog doesn't make it worse by chewing or scratching at it. Here's what to do for common, minor injuries or illnesses, and how to recognize and deal with emergencies.

Cuts and Scrapes: For a cut or scrape that's half an inch or smaller, clean the wound with saline solution or warm water

JOIN OUR
ONLINE
**Club
Boxer**™

Just like with infants, puppies need a series of vaccinations
to ensure that they stay healthy during their first year of life.
Download a vaccination chart from **DogChannel.com/Club-Boxer**
that you can fill out for your Boxer.

and use tweezers to remove any splinters or other debris. Apply an antibiotic ointment. No bandage is necessary unless the wound is on a paw, which can pick up dirt when your dog walks on it. Deep cuts or those caused by glass or some other object should be treated by your veterinarian.

Cold Symptoms: Dogs don't actually get colds, but they can get illnesses that have similar symptoms, such as coughing, a runny nose or sneezing. Dogs cough for any number of reasons, from respiratory infections to inhaled irritants to congestive heart failure. Take your Boxer to the veterinarian for prolonged coughing, or coughing accompanied by labored breathing, runny eyes or nose, or bloody phlegm.

A runny nose that continues for more than several hours requires veterinary attention, as well. If your Boxer sneezes, he may have some mild nasal irritation that will resolve on its own, but frequent sneezing, especially if it's accompanied by a runny nose, may indicate anything from allergies to an infection to something stuck in the nose.

Vomiting and Diarrhea: Sometimes dogs suffer minor gastric upsets when they eat a new type of food, eat too much, eat the contents of the trash can, or become excited or anxious. Give your Boxer's stomach a rest by withholding food for 12 hours, then feed him a bland diet such as baby food or rice and chicken, gradually returning your Boxer to his normal food. Projectile vomiting, or vomiting or diarrhea that continues for more than 48 hours, is another matter. If this happens, take your Boxer to the veterinarian.

MORE HEALTHFUL HINTS

A Boxer's anal glands can cause problems if not evacuated periodically. In the wild, dogs clear their anal glands regularly to mark their territory, but in domestic dogs, this function is no longer necessary; thus, their contents can build up and clog, causing discomfort. Signs that the anal glands on either side of the anus need emptying are if a Boxer drags its rear end along the ground or keeps turning around to attend to the uncomfortable area.

While care must be taken not to cause injury, anal glands can be evacuated by pressing gently on either side of the anal opening and by using a piece of cotton or a tissue to collect the foul-smelling matter. If anal glands are allowed to become impacted, abscesses can form, causing pain and the need for veterinary attention.

Boxers can get into all sorts of mischief, so it is not uncommon for them to swallow something poisonous. Obviously, an urgent visit to your vet is required under such circumstances, but if possible, when you telephone your vet, let him know which poisonous substance your Boxer puppy ingested, as different treatments are needed. Should it be necessary to induce vomiting (which is not always the case with poisoning), a small lump of baking soda, given orally, will have an instantaneous effect. Furthermore, a small teaspoon of salt or mustard that is dissolved in water will have a similar effect but may be more difficult to administer and may not produce results quickly.

Boxer puppies often have painful fits while they are teething. These are not usually serious and are considerably brief, caused only by the pain of teething. Of course, you must be certain that the cause is not more serious. Giving your puppy something hard to chew on will usually solve this temporary problem. If not, consult your veterinarian.

No matter how careful you are with your precious Boxer, some-times unexpected injuries happen. Be prepared for any emergency by creating a canine first-aid kit. Find out what essentials you need on **DogChannel.com/Club-Boxer** — click on "Downloads."

CHAPTER 7

ON THE TOPIC

OF HEALTH

Loving, loyal, stubborn, enthusiastic and self-confident, the Boxer makes a great family dog. He is good-natured and good with children, and his sturdy build allows him to play safely with the human members of his family. But while the Boxer carries the genes that help define his strapping conformation and wonderful temperament, like all breeds, species and humans, he also carries the defective genes that increases his risk for particular hereditary problems.

The Boxer is predisposed to several debilitating diseases that may cut his life short. Among them are cancer, dilated cardiomyopathy and bloat. Although in some cases their incidence is higher in the Boxer than in other breeds, it doesn't automatically mean every Boxer will die prematurely from genetic disorders. Several research projects are underway that may help prevent or better manage all three diseases, and health-conscious breeders may be able to minimize their risk through careful breeding.

BOXER HEALTH PROBLEMS

Unfortunately, there are too many conditions that appear to be prominent in Boxers, though the dedication and knowledge of breeders have limited the occurrence of many of these illnesses. For your sake, and

Did You Know?

Dogs can get many diseases from ticks, including Lyme disease, Rocky Mountain spotted fever, tick bite paralysis and many others.

Many skin irritations that your dog might develop can be prevented or reduced by employing a simple prevention regimen:

- Keep your Boxer's skin clean and dry.
- Shampoo your Boxer's regularly (especially during allergy season) with a hypoallergenic shampoo.
- Rinse the coat thoroughly.
- Practice good flea control.
- Supplement his diet with fatty acids.

the sake of the puppy that you purchase, be certain that the breeder has done his homework. Screening for the various congenital defects is the first step to ensuring a longer life for the Boxers around us. Breeders who do not feel it is necessary to test their stock are the breeders you want to avoid. Don't let a smooth-talking breeder convince you that his stock is unique and that he has never encountered any problems with his Boxers. What this breeder is really saying is, "I don't recognize any of those problems" and "I haven't screened any of my dogs."

The second step toward a healthy Boxer is your knowledge of the conditions that may affect the Boxer. There are early warning signs in many of these conditions and you should always keep a close eye on your dog.

CANCER CONCERNS

Perhaps the most disheartening disease that Boxer breeders and owners contend with is cancer, which comes in many forms. Breeders must screen their stock for cancers, though it is difficult to be certain since so much about cancer is still being discovered. The breed can be prone to both malignant and benign forms; the most common form of malignant cancer is a mast-cell tumor.

HEART HEALTH

The second condition that Boxers often suffer from concerns the heart. The defect known as dilated cardiomyopathy affects the heart muscles, causing heart failure in Boxers. Like a balloon, the muscles of the heart become thin and stretched, keeping the heart from functioning properly and pumping blood efficiently. Although cardiomyopathy affects other breeds, Boxers have a genetic predisposition, making it essential for Boxer breeders to screen their stock before breeding.

Smart Boxer owners should keep their eyes open for early warning signs that might include weakness, difficulty breathing, moping, coughing, difficulty with vigorous activity, lack or loss of appetite, increased heart rate and possibly fainting.

Veterinary examinations are essential, because in worst-case scenarios there are no signs. This is especially true in this breed. Dilated cardiomyopathy can be positively identified by your veterinarian, and although there is no cure presently, many Boxers respond well to therapies that include dietary supplements.

Less prevalent in this Working breed is aortic stenosis, another heart condition that involves aortic valve obstruction. It affects young puppies and is genetically transmitted in Boxers.

BLOAT

Bloat claims more lives of Boxers than anyone would like to admit. In fact, purebred dogs in general are three or four times as likely to be affected than mixed breeds. This condition, which is not believed to be congenital, occurs in deep-chested dogs like the Boxer. Also called gastric torsion, dilatation or volvulus by veterinarians, bloat refers to the condition in which the stomach fills up with air (which the dog swallows). The stomach then twists, blocking the flow of food and blood from entering or exiting the organ, and often causing death as toxins are released into the dog's bloodstream. Approximately one-third of the dogs who suffer from bloat do not recover.

While the condition is not entirely avoidable, there are a number of precautions smart owners can take to protect their Boxers from bloat.

• Feed your adult Boxer three smaller meals per day instead of one large meal, which most dogs have the tendency to gobble up. When gulping food, a large amount of air is also swallowed, which triggers bloat. Some vets even recommend adding squeaky toys or chew bones to the dog's bowl so that the dog has to eat around them, and therefore never gulps his food (or water).

• Add water to dry kibble, and have water available during the day but never at mealtimes. Like the rule your mother told you about swimming as a child, do not let your dog exercise for one hour before or after he eats.

• Use a bowl stand to lift your dog's food so that he does not have to stretch his neck to the floor to eat. Make sure the dog is calm at mealtime. If you observe these simple daily precau-

tions, your Boxer has a better chance of a long, happy, bloat-free life.

DYSPLASIA WORRIES

As with most other medium- to large-sized dogs, Boxers are prone to joint and skeletal problems, the most common being hip dysplasia. While many Boxers are genetically susceptible to hip dysplasia, not all dogs will show signs of it. Breeders commonly have a dog X-rayed at 2 years of age, before they are bred, to determine the quality of the dog's hips. Hip dysplasia is not merely a cosmetic smear, a condition that affects the gait of show dogs; it is a serious, crippling disease that can render a beloved pet wracked with pain and lameness. Consider how vigorously your Boxer loves to play and jump! Now imagine that every step he takes causes sharp pain to spread throughout his body. No one wants to see his or her dog unable to run without discomfort. Today there are simply too many irresponsibly bred puppies — whose parents were not screened for dysplasia — who can barely keep up with their owners while walking through the park.

A similar form of dysplasia concerns the elbows. This dysplasia occurs quite suddenly, and usually causes a dog to become lame. Arthritis appears in the elbow joints due to the complex disorders that veterinarians call elbow dysplasia. As with hip dysplasia, the dogs are X-rayed for elbow dysplasia. Only dogs that have "normal" elbows should be used for breeding purposes.

OTHER ILLNESSES

The bleeding disorder known as von Willebrand's disease affects many purebred dogs, including the Boxer. This is an inherited disorder that is believed to be associated with hypothyroidism. While the incidence of von Willebrand's disease has been on the rise in recent years, there are ways of determining the amount of the vW factor in the blood.

A smart owner will be on the lookout for potential diseases and injuries in his Boxer.

Hypothyroidism, a hormonal problem that is fairly common in Boxers, usually shows up in mature dogs, usually no earlier than 5 years of age. There are few early signs that an owner would recognize, though lethargy and recurrent illness or infection have been cited, as has loss of hair. Obesity, often thought to be the most common manifestation of this condition, is seen in very few cases. Although the diagnosis of hypothyroidism is tricky, vets can treat the disease rather easily and the expense incurred is not great.

In the early 1980s, England's Boxer population was scourged by progressive axonopathy, an inherited nerve disorder that is seen exclusively in this breed. Thanks to the expertise of animal geneticist Dr. Bruce Cattanach, the mode of inheritance of PA was confirmed. Breeders in England, responsibly breeding away from affected dogs, have completely eradicated PA from Boxers. The disease is characterized by awkward rear movement in young pups, usually 6 months of age, which eventually progresses to the forequarters. Although both parents must carry the genes for PA for the pups to be affected, any carrier dog or its progeny should not be bred. The disease is not a problem in North America.

Another disease that affects the Boxer almost exclusively is known as histiocytic ulcerative colitis. Affecting dogs less than 2 years old, this inflammatory disorder of the bowels is marked by diarrhea and similar signs of colitis. A combination of antibiotics and diet helps ease sufferers, though there is no cure to this chronic condition. Because a genetic link is suspected by vets, affected dogs are not to be bred.

There are far too many hereditary conditions that affect the Boxer to describe here. Discuss any of the mentioned diseases with your veterinarian and your breeder. Responsible breeders know their lines in and out and should be able to allay your fears of the possibilities of any of these conditions in your puppy. Among the other conditions that vets recommend Boxer folk look out for are Cushing's syndrome, corneal ulcers, distichiasis, entropion, lymphosarcoma and pulmonic stenosis.

AIRBORNE ALLERGIES

Just as humans suffer from hay fever during the pollinating season, many dogs suffer from the same allergies. When the pollen count is high, your Boxer might suffer, but don't expect him to sneeze or have a runny nose like you. Dogs react to pollen allergies in the same way they react to fleas; they scratch and bite themselves. Dogs, like humans, can be tested for allergens. Discuss the testing with your vet.

AUTO-IMMUNE ILLNESS

An auto-immune illness is one in which the immune system overacts and does not recognize parts of the affected body. Instead, the immune system starts to react as if these were foreign parts and need to be destroyed. An example is rheumatoid arthritis, which occurs when the body does not recognize the joints, this leads to a very painful and damaging reaction in the joints. This has nothing to do with age, so it can occur in puppies. The wear-and-tear arthritis in older dogs is called osteoarthritis.

Lupus is another auto-immune disease affecting

dogs as well as people. It can take variable forms, affecting the kidneys, bones and the skin. It can be fatal, so it is treated with steroids, which can themselves have very significant side effects. Steroids calm down the allergic reaction to the body's tissues, which helps the lupus, but also calms down the body's reaction to real foreign substances like bacteria, and also thins the skin and bones.

FOOD ALLERGIES

Feeding your Boxer properly is very important. An incorrect diet could affect your dog's health, behavior and nervous system, possibly making a normal dog aggressive. The result of a good or bad diet is most visible in a dog's skin and coat, but internal organs are affected, too.

Dogs are allergic to many foods that are popular and recommended by breeders and veterinarians. Changing the brand of food may not eliminate the problem if the ingredient to which your Boxer is allergic is contained in the new brand.

Recognizing a food allergy can be difficult. Humans often have rashes or swelling of the lips or eyes when they eat foods they are allergic to. Dogs do not usually develop rashes, but they react the same way they do to an airborne allergy; they itch, scratch and bite. While pollen allergies and parasite bites are usually seasonal, food allergies are a year-round problem.

A food allergy diagnosis is based on a two- to four-week dietary trial with a homecooked diet excluding all other foods. The diet should consist of boiled rice or potato with a source of protein that your Boxer has never eaten before, such as fresh or frozen fish, lamb or even something as exotic as pheasant. Water has to be the only drink, and it is important that no other foods are fed during this trial.

If your dog's condition improves, try the original diet again to see if the itching resumes. If it does, then your dog is allergic to his original diet. You must find a diet that does not distress your dog's skin. Start with a commercially available hypoallergenic diet or the homemade diet that you created for the allergy trial.

Food intolerance is the inability of the dog to completely digest certain foods. This occurs because the Boxer does not have the chemicals (enzymes) necessary to digest some foodstuffs.

All puppies have the enzymes necessary to digest canine milk, but some dogs do not have the enzymes to digest cow milk, resulting in loose bowels, stomach pains and flatulence.

Dogs often do not have the enzymes to digest soy or other beans. The treatment is to exclude these foods from your Boxer's diet.

PARASITE BITES

Insect bites itch, erupt and may even become infected. Dogs have the same reaction to fleas, ticks, and/or mites. When an insect lands on you, you can whisk it away with your hand. Unfortunately, when a dog is bitten by a flea, tick or mite, he can only scratch or bite. By the time your Boxer has been bitten, the parasite has done its damage. It may also have laid eggs, which will cause further problems. The itching from parasite bites is probably due to the saliva injected into the site when the parasite sucks the dog's blood.

EXTERNAL PARASITES

Fleas: Of all the problems to which dogs are prone, none is better known and more frustrating than fleas. Flea infestation is relatively simple to cure, but it can be difficult to prevent.

To control flea infestation, you have to understand the flea's life cycle. Fleas are often thought of as a summertime problem, but today's centrally heated homes have made fleas a year-round problem. The most effective method of flea control is a two-stage approach: Kill the adult fleas, then control the development of pre-adult fleas. Unfortunately, no single active ingredient is effective against all stages of the flea life cycle.

Treating fleas should be a two-pronged attack. First, the environment needs to be treated; this includes carpets and furniture, especially your Boxer's bedding and areas underneath furniture. The environment should be treated with a household spray containing an insect growth regulator and an insecticide to kill adult fleas. Most IGRs are effective against eggs and larvae; they actually mimic the fleas' own hormones and stop the eggs and larvae from developing into adult fleas. There are currently no treatments available to attack the pupae stage of the life cycle, so the adult insecticide is used to kill the newly hatched adult fleas before they find a host. Most IGRs are active for

SMART TIP!

Brush your dog's teeth every day. Plaque colonizes on the tooth surface in as little as six to eight hours, and if not removed by brushing, forms calculus (tartar) within three to five days. Plaque and tartar cause gum disease, periodontal disease, loosening of the teeth and tooth loss. With bad cases of dental disease, bacteria from the mouth can get into the bloodstream, leading to kidney or cardiac problems — either of which are life-shortening conditions.

many months, while adult insecticides are only active for a few days.

When treating with a household spray, vacuum before applying the product. This stimulates as many pupae as possible to hatch into adult fleas. The vacuum cleaner should also be treated with an insecticide to prevent the eggs and larvae that have been collected in the vacuum bag from hatching.

The second treatment stage is to apply an adult insecticide to your dog. Traditionally, this would be a collar or a spray, but more recent innovations include digestible insecticides that poison the fleas when they ingest the dog's blood. Alternatively, there are drops that, when placed on the back of the dog's neck, spread throughout the hair and skin to kill adult fleas.

Ticks: Though not as common as fleas, ticks are found all over the tropical and temperate world. They don't bite like fleas; they harpoon. They dig their sharp *proboscis* (nose) into your Boxer's skin and drink the blood, which is their only food and drink. Ticks are controlled the same way as fleas.

The American dog tick, *Dermacentor variabilis*, may be the most common dog tick in

In young puppies, roundworms cause bloated bellies, diarrhea and vomiting, and are transmitted from the mother (through blood or milk). Affected pups will not appear as animated as normal puppies. The worms appear spaghetti-like, measuring as long as 6 inches!

Mites: Just as fleas and ticks can be problematic for your dog, mites can also lead to an itch fit. Microscopic in size, mites are related to ticks and generally take up permanent residence on their host animal — in this case, your Boxer! The term "mange" refers to any infestation caused by one of the mighty mites, of which there are six varieties that smart dog owners should know.

■ Demodex mites cause a condition known as *demodicosis* (sometimes called "red mange" or "follicular mange"), in which the mites live in the dog's hair follicles and sebaceous glands in larger-than-normal numbers. Most dogs recover from this type of mange without any treatment, though topical therapies are commonly prescribed by veterinarians.

■ The *Cheyletiellosis* mite is the hook-mouthed culprit associated with "walking dandruff," a condition that affects dogs as well as cats and rabbits. If untreated, this mange can affect a whole kennel of dogs and can be spread to humans, as well.

■ The *Sarcoptes* mite causes intense itching on the dog in the form of a condition known as scabies or sarcoptic mange. Scabies is highly contagious and can be passed to humans. Sometimes an allergic reaction to the mite worsens the severe itching associated with sarcoptic mange.

■ Ear mites, *Otodectes cynotis*, lead to otodectic mange, which commonly affects the outer ear canal of the dog, though other areas can be affected as well. Your vet can prescribe a treatment to flush out the ears and kill any eggs in the ears. A complete month of treatment is necessary to cure this variety of mange.

■ Two other mites, less common in dogs, include *Dermanyssus gallinae* (the "poultry" or "red mite") and *Eutrombicula alfreddugesi* (the North American mite associated with

many areas, especially areas where the climate is hot and humid. Most dog ticks have life expectancies of a week to 6 months, depending on climatic conditions. They can neither jump nor fly, but they can crawl slowly and can travel up to 16 feet to reach a sleeping or unsuspecting dog.

trombiculidiasis or chigger infestation). The types of mange caused by both of these mites must be treated by vets.

INTERNAL PARASITES

Most animals — fish, birds and mammals, including dogs and humans — have worms and other parasites that live inside their bodies. According to Dr. Herbert R. Axelrod, a fish pathologist, there are two kinds of parasites: dumb and smart. The smart parasites live in peaceful cooperation with their hosts (symbiosis), while dumb parasites kill their hosts. Most worm infections are relatively easy to control. If they are not controlled, they weaken the host dog to the point that other medical problems occur, but they do not kill the host as dumb parasites would.

Roundworms: Roundworms that infect dogs live in the dog's intestines and shed eggs continually. It has been estimated that a dog produces about six or more ounces of feces every day, each ounce averages hundreds of thousands of roundworm eggs when the dog is infected. There are no known areas in which dogs roam that do not contain roundworm eggs. Because roundworms infect people, too, it is wise to have your dog regularly tested.

Roundworm infection can kill puppies and cause severe problems in adult dogs, as the hatched larvae travel to the lungs and trachea through the bloodstream. Cleanliness is the best preventive for roundworms. Always pick up after your dog and dispose of feces in appropriate receptacles.

Hookworms: Hookworms are dangerous to humans as well as to dogs and cats, and can be the cause of severe iron-deficiency anemia. The worm uses its teeth to attach itself to the dog's intestines and changes its attachment site about six times per day. Each

time the worm repositions itself, the dog loses blood and can become anemic.

Symptoms of hookworm infection include dark stools, weight loss, general weakness, pale coloration and anemia, as well as possible skin problems. Fortunately, hookworms are easily purged with a number of medications that have proven effective. Discuss these with your veterinarian. Most heartworm preventives include a hookworm insecticide, as well.

Humans, can be infected by hookworms through exposure to contaminated feces. Because the worms cannot complete their life cycle on a human, the worms simply infest the skin and cause irritation. As a preventive, use disposable gloves or a poop-scoop to pick up your dog's droppings and prevent your dog (or neighborhood cats) from defecating in children's play areas.

Tapeworms: There are many species of tapeworm, all of which are carried by fleas! Fleas are so small that your Boxer could pass them onto your hands, your plate or your food, making it possible for you to ingest a flea that is carrying tapeworm eggs. While tapeworm infection is not life-threatening in dogs (smart parasite!), it can be the cause of a very serious liver disease in humans.

Whipworms: In North America, whipworms are counted among the most common parasitic worms in dogs. Affected dogs may only experience upset tummies, colic and diarrhea. These worms, however, can

live for months or years in the dog, beginning their larval stage in the small intestine, spending their adult stage in the large intestine and finally passing infective eggs through the dog's feces. The only way to detect whipworms is through a fecal examination, though this is not always foolproof. Treatment for whipworms is tricky, due to the worms' unusual life cycle, and often dogs are reinfected due to exposure to infective eggs on the ground. Cleaning up droppings in your backyard as well as in public places is absolutely essential for sanitation purposes and the health of your dog and others.

Threadworms: Though less common than roundworms, hookworms and the aforementioned parasites, threadworms concern dog owners in the southwestern United

States and the Gulf Coast area where the climate is hot and humid.

Living in a dog's small intestine, this worm measures a mere two millimeters and is round in shape. Like the whipworm, the threadworm's life cycle is very complex, and the eggs and larvae are passed through the feces.

A deadly disease in humans, threadworms readily infect people, mostly through handling feces. Threadworms are most often seen in young puppies. The most common symptoms include bloody diarrhea and pneumonia. Sick puppies must be isolated and treated immediately; vets recommend a follow-up treatment one month later.

Heartworms: Heartworms are thin, extended worms up to 12 inches long, that live in a dog's heart and the major blood vessels surrounding it. Dogs can have up to 200 heartworms. Symptoms may be loss of energy, loss of appetite, coughing, the development of a pot belly and anemia.

Heartworms are transmitted by mosquitoes, which drink the blood of infected dogs and take in larvae with the blood. The larvae, called *microfilariae*, develop within the body of the mosquito and are passed on to the next dog bitten after the larvae mature. It takes two to three weeks for the larvae to develop to the infective stage within the body of the mosquito. Dogs are usually treated at about 6 weeks of age and maintained on a prophylactic dose given monthly.

Blood testing for heartworms is not necessarily indicative of how seriously your dog is infected. Although this is a dangerous disease, it is not easy for a dog to be infected. Discuss various prevention methods with your vet because there are many different types now available. Together you can decide on a safe course of prevention for your Boxer.

Many health problems come from parasites — external and internal. Keep your Boxer and his areas clean to prevent both.

DIET

You have probably heard it a thousand times: You are what you eat. Believe it or not, it is very true. For dogs, they are what you feed them because they have little choice in the matter. Even smart owners who truly want to feed their Boxers only the best often can't do so because they do not know which foods are best for their dogs.

BASIC TYPES

Dog foods are produced in various types: dry, wet (canned), semimoist and frozen.

Dry dog food is useful for cost-conscious owners because it tends to be less expensive than the others. These foods contain the least fat and the most preservatives. Dry food is bulky and takes longer to eat than other foods, so it's more filling.

Wet food — available in both cans and foil pouches — is usually 60 to 70 percent water and is more expensive than dry food. A palatable source of concentrated nutrition, wet food makes a good supplement for underweight dogs or those recovering from illness. Some smart owners add a little wet food to dry food to increase its appeal, and their dogs gobble up this tasty mixture.

it's a **Fact**

Bones can cause gastrointestinal obstruction and perforation and may be contaminated with salmonella or E. coli. Leave them in the trash and give your dog a nylon bone instead.

Semimoist food is flavorful but usually contains a lot of sugar, which can lead to dental problems and obesity. It's not a good choice for your dog's main diet.

Frozen food, available in cooked and raw forms, is usually more expensive than wet foods. The advantages of frozen food are similar to those of wet foods.

The amount of food your Boxer needs depends on a number of factors, such as age, activity level, food quality, reproductive status and size. What's the easiest way to figure it out? Start with the manufacturer's recommended amount, then adjust it according to your dog's response. For example, feed the recommended amount for a few weeks and if your Boxer loses weight, increase the amount by 10 to 20 percent. If your dog gains weight, decrease the amount. It won't take long to determine how much food keeps your best friend in optimal condition.

NUTRITION 101

All Boxers (and all dogs, for that matter) need nutrients like proteins, carbohydrates, fats, vitamins and minerals for optimal growth and health.

■ **Proteins** are used for growth and repair of muscles, bones and other bodily tissues. They're also used for production of antibodies, enzymes and hormones. All dogs need protein, but it's especially important for puppies because they grow and develop so rapidly. Protein sources include various types of meat, meat meal, meat byproducts, eggs, dairy products and soybeans.

■ **Carbohydrates** are metabolized into glucose, the body's energy source. Carbohydrates are available as sugars, starches and fiber.

• Sugars (monosaccharides) are not suitable nutrient sources for dogs.

• Starches — a preferred type of carbohydrate in dog food — are found in a variety of plant products. Starches must be cooked to be digested.

• Fiber — also a preferred type of carbohydrates in dog food — isn't digestible, but helps the digestive tract function properly.

■ **Fats** are also used for energy and play an important role in skin and coat health, hormone production, nervous system function and vitamin transport. Fat increases the palatability and the calorie count of puppy/dog food, too much of which can lead to serious health problems, such as obesity. Some foods contain added amounts of omega fatty acids in the form of docosohexaenoic acid, a compound that may enhance both brain development and learning in puppies but is not considered an essential nutrient by the Association of American Feed Control Officials (www.aafco.org). Fats used in dog foods include sources such as tallow, lard, poultry fat, fish oil and vegetable oils.

Believe it or not, during your Boxer's lifetime, you'll buy a few thousand pounds of dog food! Go to **DogChannel.com/Club-Boxer** and download a chart that outlines the cost of dog food.

■ **Vitamins** and **minerals** participate in muscle and nerve function, bone growth, healing, metabolism and fluid balance. Calcium, phosphorus and vitamin D supplied in the right amounts are especially important for your puppy to ensure proper bone and teeth development.

Water is as essential as proper nutrition. Water keeps your Boxer's body properly hydrated and promotes normal body system functions. During housetraining, it is necessary to keep an eye on how much water your Boxer is drinking. Once reliably trained, he should have access to clean, fresh water at all times, especially if you feed him dry food. Make sure the water bowl is clean and change the water often.

CHECK OUT THE LABEL

To help you get a feel for what you are feeding your Boxer, start by taking a look at the label on the package or can. Look for the words "complete and balanced." This will tell you that the food meets specific nutritional requirements set by the AAFCO for either adults ("maintenance") or puppies and pregnant/lactating females ("growth and reproduction"). The label must state the group for which it is intended. If you're feeding a puppy, choose a "growth and reproduction" food.

The food label also includes a nutritional analysis, which lists minimum protein, minimum fat, maximum fiber and maximum moisture content, as well as other information. (You won't find carbohydrate content because it's everything that isn't protein, fat, fiber and moisture.)

The nutritional analysis refers to crude protein and crude fat — amounts that have been determined in the laboratory. This analysis is technically accurate, but it doesn't tell you anything about digestibility: how much of the particular nutrient your Boxer can actually use. For information about digestibility, contact the manufacturer (check the label for a phone number or website).

Virtually all commercial puppy foods exceed AAFCO's minimal requirements for protein and fat, the two nutrients most commonly evaluated when comparing foods. Protein levels in dry puppy foods usually range from about 26 to 30 percent; for canned foods, the values are about 9 to 13 percent. The fat content of dry puppy foods is about 20 percent or more; for canned foods, it's 8 percent or more. Dry food values are larger than canned food values because dry food contains less water; the values are actually similar when compared on a dry matter basis.

Dogs of all ages love treats and table food, but these goodies can unbalance your Boxer's diet and lead to a weight problem if you don't choose and feed her wisely. Table food, whether fed as a treat or as part of a meal, shouldn't account for more than 10 percent of your Boxer's daily caloric intake. If you plan to give your dog treats, be sure to include "treat calories" when calculating the daily food requirement — so you don't end up with a pudgy pup!

When shopping for packaged treats, look for ones that provide complete nutrition. They're basically dog food in a fun form. Choose crunchy goodies for chewing fun and dental health. Other ideas for tasty treats include:

✓ small chunks of cooked, lean meat
✓ dry dog food morsels
✓ cheese
✓ veggies (cooked, raw or frozen)
✓ breads, crackers or dry cereal
✓ unsalted, unbuttered, plain, popped popcorn

Some foods, however, can be dangerous or even deadly to your dog. The following can cause digestive upset (vomiting or diarrhea) or toxic reactions that could be fatal:

✗ **avocados:** This popular fruit an cause gastrointestinal irritation, with vomiting and diarrhea, if your dog eats it in sufficient quantity

✗ **baby food:** may contain onion powder and does not provide balanced nutrition

✗ **chocolate:** contains methylxanthines and theobromine, caffeine-like compounds that can cause vomiting, diarrhea, heart abnormalities, tremors, seizures and death. Darker chocolates contain higher levels of the toxic compounds.

✗ **eggs, raw:** Whites contain an enzyme that prevents uptake of biotin, a B vitamin; may contain salmonella.

✗ **garlic (and related foods):** can cause gastrointestinal irritation and anemia if eaten in sufficient quantity

✗ **grapes:** can cause kidney failure if eaten in sufficient quantity (the toxic dose varies from dog to dog)

✗ **macadamia nuts:** can cause vomiting, weakness, lack of coordination and other problems

✗ **meat, raw:** may contain harmful bacteria such as salmonella or *E. coli*

✗ **milk:** can cause diarrhea in some puppies

✗ **onions (and related foods):** can cause gastrointestinal irritation and anemia if eaten in sufficient quantity

✗ **raisins:** can cause kidney failure if eaten in sufficient quantity (the toxic dose varies from dog to dog)

✗ **yeast bread dough:** can rise in the gastrointestinal tract, causing obstruction; produces alcohol as it rises

Finally, check the ingredients on the label, which lists the ingredients in descending order by weight. Manufacturers are allowed to list separately different forms of a single ingredient (e.g., ground corn and corn gluten meal). The food may contain things like meat byproducts, meat and bone meal, and animal fat, which probably won't appeal to you but are nutritious and safe for your puppy. Higher quality foods usually have meat or meat products near the top of the ingredient list, but you don't need to worry about grain products as long as the label indicates that the food is nutritionally complete. Dogs are omnivores (not carnivores, as commonly believed), so all balanced dog foods contain animal and plant ingredients.

Don't feed your Boxer from the table. Do it once, and he will always expect it.

STAGES OF LIFE

When selecting your dog's diet, three stages of development must be considered: the puppy stage, the adult stage and the senior stage.

Puppy Diets: Pups instinctively want to nurse, a normal puppy will exhibit this behavior from just a few moments following birth. Puppies should be allowed to nurse for about the first six weeks, although from the third or fourth week, the breeder will begin to introduce small portions of suitable solid food. Most breeders like to introduce alternate milk and meat meals initially, building up to weaning time.

By the time the puppies are 7 or a maximum of 8 weeks old, they should be fully weaned and fed solely on a proprietary puppy food. Selection of the most suitable, good-quality diet at this time is essential, for a puppy's fastest growth rate is during the first year of life. Seek advice about your

Smaller puppy bellies mean more refills. Feed your puppy several times a day to keep his energy up.

Feeding your dog is part of your daily routine. Take a break, and have some fun online and play "Feed the Boxer," an exclusive game found only on **DogChannel.com/Club-Boxer** — just click on "Games."

How can you tell if your Boxer is fit or fat? When you run your hands down your pal's sides from front to back, you should be able to easily feel her ribs. It's OK if you feel a little body fat (and, of course, a lot of hair), but you should not feel huge fat pads. You should also be able to feel your Boxer's waist — an indentation behind the ribs.

dog's food from your veterinarian. The frequency of meals will be reduced over time, and when a young dog has reached the age of about 10 to 12 months, he should be switched to an adult diet.

Puppy and junior diets can be well balanced for the needs of your Boxer so, except in certain circumstances, additional vitamins, minerals and proteins will not be required.

How many times a day does your Boxer need to eat? Puppies have small stomachs and high metabolic rates, so they need to eat several times a day in order to obtain sufficient nutrients. If your Boxer puppy is younger than 3 months old, feed him four or five meals a day. When your little buddy is 3 to 5 months old, decrease the number of meals to three or four. At 6 months of age, most puppies can move to an adult schedule of two meals a day.

Adult Diets: A dog is considered an adult when he has stopped growing. Rely on your veterinarian or dietary specialist to recommend an acceptable maintenance diet. Major dog food manufacturers specialize in this type of food, and smart owners must select the one best suited to their Boxer's needs. Do not leave food out all day for free-feeding, as this freedom inevitably translates to increased inches around the dog's waist.

Senior Diets: As dogs get older, their metabolism changes. The older Boxer usually exercises less, moves more slowly and sleeps more. This change in lifestyle and physiological performance requires a change in diet. Because these changes take place slowly, they might not be so easily

Your Boxer can't read labels so he looks to you to provide healthy and nutritious meals.

recognizable. These metabolic changes increase the tendency toward obesity, requiring an even more vigilant approach to feeding. Obesity in an older dog compounds the health problems that already accompany old age.

As your Boxer gets older, few of his organs function up to par. The kidneys slow down, and the intestines become less efficient. These age-related factors are best handled with a change in diet and a change in feeding schedule to give smaller portions that are more easily digested.

There is no single best diet for every older dog. While many older dogs will do perfectly fine on light or senior diets, other dogs will do better on special premium

Did You Know?

Because semi-moist food contains lots of sugar, it isn't a good selection for your Boxer's main menu. However, it is great for an occasional yummy snack. Try forming it into little balls for a once-a-week treat! It's easy, and she'll love ya for it!

diets such as lamb and rice. Be sensitive about your senior Boxer's diet, and this may help control other problems that may arise with your old friend.

These delicious, dog-friendly recipes will have your furry friend smacking her lips and salivating for more. Just remember: Treats aren't meant to replace your dog's regular meals. Give your Boxer snacks sparingly and continue to feed her nutritious, well-balanced meals.

Cheddar Squares

$\frac{1}{3}$ cup all-natural applesauce
$\frac{1}{3}$ cup low-fat cheddar cheese, shredded
$\frac{1}{3}$ cup water
2 cups unbleached white flour

In a medium bowl, mix the first three ingredients. In a large bowl, measure the flour. Slowly add all the wet ingredients to the flour.

Mix well. Pour batter into a greased 13x9x2-inch pan. Bake at 375-degrees Fahrenheit for 25 to 30 minutes. Bars are done when a toothpick inserted in the center comes out clean. Cool and cut into bars. This recipe makes about 54, $1\frac{1}{2}$-inch bars.

Peanut Butter Bites

3 tablespoons vegetable oil
$\frac{1}{4}$ cup smooth peanut butter, no salt or sugar
$\frac{1}{4}$ cup honey
$1\frac{1}{2}$ teaspoon baking powder
2 eggs
2 cups whole wheat flour

In a large bowl, mix all ingredients until dough is firm. If the dough is too sticky, mix in a small amount of flour. Knead dough on a lightly floured surface until firm. Roll out dough until it is half an inch thick and cut with cookie cutters. Put cookies on a cookie sheet half an inch apart. Bake at 350-degrees Fahrenheit for 20 to 25 minutes. When done, cookies should be firm to the touch. Turn oven off and leave cookies for one to two hours to harden. This recipe makes about 40, 2-inch-long cookies.

CHAPTER 9

FOR A BEAUTIFUL

BOXER

I f you're in and out of the shower in 10 minutes and you don't want a dog that requires more primping than you do, the Boxer just might be the breed for you.

Keep in mind, though, that although these are wash-and-wear dogs, their short coats do shed, and they do have basic grooming needs that must be maintained. While the adult Boxer revels in the attention of being groomed, he only requires grooming sessions every two weeks and bathing every six weeks.

GEAR UP

No matter what the television commercial models with long, flowing tresses tell you, the ingredients you add externally to your pet's hair will not change a brittle, lifeless coat into a soft, healthy one. The truth is that if you want your Boxer to have a healthy coat, then take a close look at your dog's nutrition. Healthy hair and skin begins with good nutrition, and a good premium dog food is the best place to start. Your pet's diet is not the place to economize. Purchase the best food you can afford and resist the impulse to save money at

Did You Know?

Nail clipping can be tricky, so many dog owners leave the task for professional groomers. However, if you walk your Boxer on concrete often, you may not have to worry about it. The concrete acts like a nail file and probably will keep your dog's nails in check.

your Boxer's expense. Boxers' skin can be sensitive, so consult your veterinarian when choosing your dog's diet. Once you've established a good nutritional base, you can move on to improving your pet's coat from the outside.

In order to keep your Boxer polished, you will need some grooming essentials:

- a pair of nail clippers
- styptic powder
- cotton balls
- ear powder or cleaner
- tearless pet shampoo
- a coat conditioner
- hydrogen peroxide or some baby wipes
- a rubber curry brush

BATH AND BRUSH

Boxers only need to be bathed once every six to eight weeks or so – or when they find a mud puddle to their liking. Bathing them too often removes natural oils from the coat. Some groomers prefer a high-quality medicated shampoo, which helps keep the skin in better condition, while many avoid products containing tea tree oil.

Washing, rather than scrubbing the coat, minimizes the possibility of stripping coat oils or irritating sensitive skin. After completely wetting your Boxer, saturate a large bath sponge with shampoo and gently glide it over your dog's entire coat. Do not pour the shampoo directly onto your dog. Work in the direction of the hair growth, and do not rub or scrub. Rinse and repeat. A conditioning rinse is not recommended because it may soften the coat's natural texture. The final rinse should leave the coat squeaky clean. Make sure that no soap residue remains in the coat. If your Boxer's skin seems itchy or flaky the day after a bath, this is often due to inadequate rinsing.

The key to a successful bath is organization. Keep all your grooming tools in a basket so you can set up for the bath in only a moment. (This comes in handy when your zestful Boxer finds something interesting in the yard to roll in and you need to move quickly!)

Check the temperature of the water against the inside of your wrist or with your hand. Once you reach the temperature you desire, hold the hose close to your dog's body to eliminate excessive spray. If you do not have a hose attachment, use a cup to scoop water and pour it over your dog.

Work from the highest to the lowest point on your dog with the water and shampoo; use your fingers to work the shampoo throughout the coat.

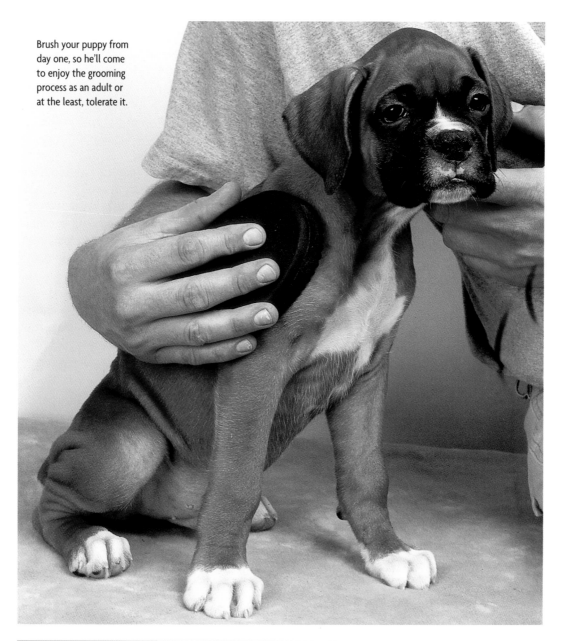

Brush your puppy from day one, so he'll come to enjoy the grooming process as an adult or at the least, tolerate it.

After removing a tick, clean your dog's skin with hydrogen peroxide. If Lyme disease is common where you live, have your veterinarian test the tick. Tick preventive medication will discourage ticks from attaching and kill any that do. — groomer Andrea Vilardi from West Paterson, N.J.

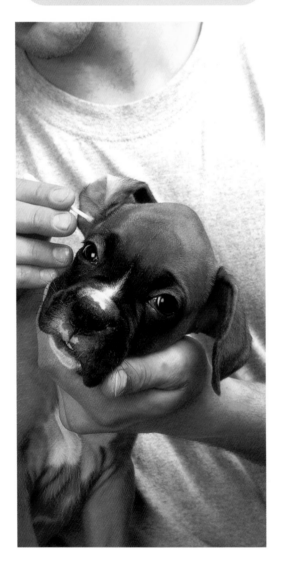

it's a Fact

Boxers shed minimally year-round and many experience pronounced seasonal shedding in the spring and fall. Seasonal shedding is more evident in climates with definite seasons because light has a large effect on coat growth.

To keep water from getting into the nose when you rinse this area, hold your hand as a barrier around the nose and let the water flow from behind your Boxer's ears toward your hand and break the water against your hand. Rinse your dog with a gentle flow of water until the hair feels clean and the water runs clear.

When drying the coat, use a blotting technique, squeezing the hair instead of rubbing the towel back and forth, to prevent matting. If you use a hair dryer, test the air flow against the inside of your wrist first, then hold it about 10 to 12 inches from the dog.

BRUSH THAT HAIR

Regular brushing, at least once a week, also contributes to healthy skin. The rubber curry brush comes in many varieties. A favorite is an oval rubber brush with serrated edges. Used to massage the coat with the lie of the hair, it gently whisks away dead hair, and most dogs love the attention. A grooming mitt with little rubber nubs works equally well, and some enthusiasts swear by a chamois cloth to add luster to that gleaming coat. Some breeders use pumice stone to remove dead hair, leaving the gleaming body coat smooth as glass. Pumice stone is available at suppliers' booths at dog shows and through some catalogs. Use only prior to a bath as it leaves an odor on the coat.

Because the Boxer has a short muzzle, prominent dewlaps and facial folds, a daily face wash with a damp washcloth is a good idea. Some of these dogs also tend to "slobber" when excited, so daily cleansing prevents odor from saliva and keeps the face free of debris from food, dust and pollen. Excessive salivation could indicate a dental infection or signal an illness and a health checkup would be warranted.

At the end of every coat growth cycle, hair dies and leaves the coat looking dull and lifeless until dead hair is shed and new hair emerges. Frequent brushing speeds up the process and stimulates regrowth from each hair follicle.

NOW EAR THIS

Whether your Boxer has cropped or natural ears, they should be checked frequently and cleaned at least once a week. Cropped ears permit better air circulation, but there is a bigger risk of water or debris getting into the ear canal. Ear infections can become serious before you notice anything is wrong. Symptoms of an ear problem include sensitivity to touch, heavy buildup of wax and debris, inflammation, odor, head shaking/scratching or head tilting. Bacterial, fungal or yeast infections may require veterinary treatment.

Moisture is a major source of infection; you can put cotton in your dog's ears before a bath to prevent water from getting into the ear canals. Ears should always be swabbed and dried carefully after swimming or bathing.

The canine ear canal makes an abrupt turn near the jaw, creating an ideal setting for potential infections. Ear cleaning solution not only helps flush out debris, it restores the ear's pH levels to discourage infection. Squirt enough ear cleaning solution into the ear to fill the canal and gently massage the opening for a few seconds to loosen debris. Use a cotton ball to wipe away all visible moisture, earwax and dirt.

NAIL TRIMMING

Immediately after the bath is the best time to clip the nails because the water has softened the nails and your Boxer may be somewhat tired-out by the bath. Nail

JOIN OUR
ONLINE
Club
Boxer™

Every Boxer should look ready for the ring — the show ring, that is. What do you need to keep your pup looking his best? Go to Club Boxer (**DogChannel.com/Club-Boxer**) and download a checklist of essential grooming equipment you will need.

trimming is recommended every two weeks with nail clippers or a nail grinding tool. Short nails are crucial to maintaining the breed's normal foot shape. Long nails will permanently damage any dog's feet, the tight ligaments of round, arched feet will break down more quickly. If your dog's nails are clicking on the floor, they need trimming.

When grinding, use a low-speed (5,000 to 10,000 rpm) cordless nail grinder fitted with a fine grade (100 grit) sandpaper cylinder. Stone cylinders are more prone to heat buildup and vibration. Hold the dog's paw firmly in one hand, spreading the toes slightly. Touch the spinning grinder wheel to the nail tip for one or two seconds without applying pressure. Repeat if necessary to remove only the nail tip protruding beyond the quick. Grinders have the added benefit of leaving nails smooth and free of sharp, jagged edges produced by traditional nail clippers.

Your Boxer should be accustomed to having his nails trimmed at an early age, because it will be part of your maintenance routine throughout his life. Not only do trim nails appear nicer, they're safer. Long nails

can unintentionally scratch someone, and they have a better chance of ripping, bleeding or causing the feet to spread.

Before you start cutting, make sure you can identify the "quick" (the vein in the center of each nail). It will bleed if accidentally cut, which will be quite painful for the dog as it contains nerve endings. Keep some type of clotting agent on hand, such as a styptic pencil or powder (the type used for shaving). This will stop the bleeding quickly when applied to the end of the cut nail. Do not panic if this happens, just stop the bleeding and talk soothingly to your Boxer. Once he has calmed down, move on to the next nail. It is better to clip a little at a time, particularly with black-nailed dogs.

Hold your pup steady as you begin trimming his nails; you do not want him to make any sudden movements or run away. Talk to him soothingly and stroke him as you clip. Holding his foot in your hand, simply take off the end of each nail in one quick clip. You can purchase nail clippers that are specially made for dogs; you can probably find them wherever you buy grooming supplies.

There are two predominant types of clippers. One is the guillotine clipper, which is a hole with a blade in the middle. Squeeze the handles, and the blade meets the nail and chops it off. For some dogs, it is intolerable. Scissor-type clippers are gentler on the nail. Make sure the blades on either of these clippers are sharp. Once you are at the desired length, use a nail file to smooth the rough

edges so they don't catch on carpeting or outdoor debris.

If the procedure becomes more than you can deal with, just remember: Groomers and veterinarians charge a nominal fee to clip nails. By using their services you won't have to see your pet glower at you for the rest of the night.

When inspecting paws, you must check not only the nails but also the pads. Take care that the pads have not become cracked, and always check between the pads to be sure nothing has become lodged there. Depending on the season, there may be a

Don't think of grooming sessions as a chore. Make them fun and enjoyable with treats and lots of petting.

danger of grass seeds or thorns becoming embedded, even tar from the road could get stuck. Butter, by the way, is useful to help remove tar from your Boxer's paws.

THE TOPIC OF TEETH

Like people, Boxers can suffer from dental disease, so experts recommend regular tooth brushing. Daily brushing is best, but your dog will benefit from tooth brushing a few times a week. Teeth should be white and free of yellowish tartar and the gums should appear healthy and pink. Gums that bleed easily when you perform dental duties may have gingivitis.

The first thing to know is that your pup probably won't want your fingers in his mouth. Desensitizing your puppy — getting him to accept that you will be looking at and touching his teeth — is the first step to overcoming his reticence. You can begin this as soon as you get your puppy, with the help of the thing that motivates him most: food.

For starters, let your puppy lick some chicken, vegetable or beef broth off your finger. Then, dip your finger in broth again, and gently insert your finger in the side of your dog's mouth. Touch his side teeth and gums. Several sessions will get your puppy used to having his mouth touched.

Boxers don't need a lot of maintenance to look like champions.

Use a dog toothbrush or fingertip brush to brush your Boxer's teeth. Hold the mouth with one hand and brush with the other. Use toothpaste made specifically for dogs with dog-slurping flavors like poultry and beef. The human kind froths too much and can give your dog an upset stomach. Brush in a circular motion with the brush held at a 45-degree angle to the gum line. Be sure to get the fronts, tops and sides of each tooth.

Look for signs of plaque, tartar or gum disease, including redness, swelling, foul breath, discolored enamel near the gum line and receding gums. If you see these, take your dog to the veterinarian immediately. Also see your vet about once a year for a dental checkup.

REWARD A JOB WELL DONE

Rewarding your Boxer for good behaving during grooming is the best way to ensure stress-free sessions. Bathing energizes him, and using the time immediately after grooming as play time is the best way to reward your Boxer for a job well done.

Watching your clean, healthy Boxer tear from room to room in sheer joy is your reward for being a caring owner.

Six Tips for Boxer Care

1. Grooming tools can be scary to some dogs, so let your dog see and sniff everything at the onset. Keep your beauty sessions short, too. Most Boxers don't enjoy standing still for too long.
2. Look at your dog's eyes for any discharge and her ears for inflammation, debris or foul odor. If you notice anything that doesn't look right, contact your veterinarian ASAP.
3. Choose a time to groom your dog when you don't have to rush and assemble all of the grooming tools before you begin. This way you can focus on your Boxer's needs instead of having to stop in the middle of the session.
4. Start establishing a grooming routine the day after you bring her home. A regular grooming schedule will make it easier to remember what touch-up tasks your dog needs.
5. Proper nail care helps with your dog's gait and spinal alignment. Nails that are too long can force a dog to walk improperly. Also, too-long nails can snag and tear, causing painful injury to your Boxer.
6. Good dental health prevents gum disease and early tooth loss. Brush your Boxer's teeth daily, and see a veterinarian yearly.

Six Questions to Ask a Groomer

1. Do you cage dry? Are you willing to hand dry or air dry my dog?
2. What type of shampoo are you using? Is it tearless? If not, do you have a tearless variety available for use?
3. Will you restrain my pet if she acts up for nail-clipping? What methods do you use for difficult dogs?
4. Are you familiar with Boxers? Do you have any references from other Boxer owners?
5. Is the shop air-conditioned in hot weather?
6. Will my dog be getting brushed or just bathed?

TRAIN

To bring out the best in your Boxer, teach him with firm and fair training methods. Start when he's young — as soon as you bring him home. Waiting until he's 6 months old is a serious waste of good training time; at that age, he'll be much larger and more difficult to control.

In contrast, an 8- to 12-week-old puppy is a more manageable size and soaks up everything you teach him. Look into the future and recognize that what's cute and harmless at 8 weeks of age won't be at all cute and harmless at 8 months. That vision of what's to come should be more than enough to motivate you to start training your Boxer early, at home and in a puppy kindergarten class.

Your young Boxer puppy can easily learn the training cues sit, down and stay. By the time he's 4 months old, he can be doing extended versions of these cues. All it takes is positive motivation — the use of food, treats and toys — and gentle guidance with your hands to show him the moves or restrain him as necessary. With puppies, use motivational techniques such as luring (using a treat to

Did You Know?

The prime period for socialization is short. Most behavior experts agree that positive experiences during the 10-week period between 4 and 14 weeks of age are vital to the development of a puppy who'll grow into an adult Boxer with a sound temperament.

lure the dog into a position) and shaping (rewarding small pieces of a behavior until you get the whole thing) certain behaviors, such as sit and down, through the use of a marker word or sound, such as a clicker.

Reward-based training methods — clicking and luring — show dogs what to do and help them do it correctly, setting them up for success and rewards rather than mistakes and punishment. Most dogs find food rewards meaningful — Boxers are no exception. They tend to be very food-motivated. This works well because positive training relies on using treats, at least initially, to encourage your dog to demonstrate a behavior. The treat is then given as a reward. When you reinforce desired behaviors with rewards that are valuable to your dog, you are met with happy cooperation rather than resistance.

A training harness is a better choice than a collar. It allows you more control over your Boxer.

Positive reinforcement does not mean permissive. While you are rewarding your Boxer's desirable behaviors, you must manage him to be sure he doesn't get rewarded for his undesirable behaviors. Training tools, such as leashes, tethers, baby gates and crates, will help keep your dog out of trouble. Force-free negative punishment (the dog's behavior makes a good thing go away) will help him realize there are negative consequences for inappropriate behaviors.

LEARNING SOCIAL GRACES

Now that you have done all of the preparatory work and have helped your Boxer get accustomed to his new home and family, it is time for you to have some fun! Socializing your tiny pup gives you the opportunity to show off your new friend, and

SMART TIP!

If your Boxer refuses to sit with both haunches squarely beneath her and instead sits on one side or the other, she may have a physical reason for doing so. Discuss the habit with your veterinarian to be certain that your dog isn't suffering from some structural problem.

your Boxer gets to reap the benefits of being an adorable little creature who people will want to pet and, in general, think is absolutely precious!

Besides getting to know his new family, your puppy should be exposed to other people, animals and situations, but, of course, he must not come into close contact with dogs who you don't know until he has had all his vaccinations. Constant interaction will help him become well-adjusted as he grows up and less prone to being timid or fearful of the new things he will encounter.

Your pup's socialization began at the breeder's home, but now it is your responsibility to continue it. The socialization he receives up until 12 weeks is the most critical, as this is the time when he forms his impressions of the outside world. Be especially careful during the 8- to 10-week period, also known as the fear period. The interaction he receives during this time should be gentle and reassuring. Lack of socialization can manifest itself in fear and aggression as your dog matures. A puppy needs lots of human contact, affection, handling and exposure to other animals.

Once your Boxer has received his necessary vaccinations, feel free to take him out and about (on his leash, of course). Walk him around the neighborhood, take him on your daily errands, let people pet him and let him meet other dogs and pets. Make sure to

Training works best when blended into daily life. When your Boxer asks for something — food, play, whatever — cue her to do something for you first. Reward her by granting her request. Practice in different settings, so she learns to listen regardless of her surroundings.

expose your Boxer to different people — men, women, kids, babies, men with beards, teenagers with cell phones or riding skateboards, joggers, shoppers, someone in a wheelchair, a pregnant woman, etc. Make sure your Boxer explores different surfaces like sidewalks, gravel and a puddle. Positive experience is the key to building confidence. It's up to you to make sure your Boxer safely discovers the world so he will be a calm, confident and well-socialized dog.

It's important that you take the lead in all socialization experiences and never put your pup in a scary or potentially harmful situation. Be mindful of your Boxer's limitations. Fifteen minutes at a public market is fine; two hours at a loud outdoor concert is too much. Meeting vaccinated, tolerant and gentle older dogs is great. Meeting dogs who you don't know isn't a great idea, especially if they appear very energetic, dominant or fearful. Control the situations in which you place your Boxer.

The best way to socialize your puppy to a new experience is to make him think it's the best thing ever. You can do this with a lot of happy talk, enthusiasm and, yes, food. To convince your puppy that almost any experience is a blast, always carry treats. Consider carrying two types — a bag of his puppy chow, which you can give when introducing him to nonthreatening experiences, and a bag of high-value, mouth-watering treats to give him when introducing him to scarier experiences.

BASIC CUES

All Boxers, regardless of your training and relationship goals, need to know at least five basic good-manner behaviors: sit, down, stay, come and heel. Here are tips for teaching your dog these important cues.

SIT: Every dog should learn how to sit.

- Hold a treat at the end of your dog's nose.
- Move the treat over his head.
- When he sits, click a clicker or say "Yes!"
- Feed your dog the treat.
- If your dog jumps up, hold the treat lower. If he backs up, back him into a corner and wait until he sits. Be patient. Keep your clicker handy and click (or say "Yes!") and treat anytime he offers a sit.
- When he easily offers sits, say "sit" just before he offers, so he can make the association between the word and the behavior. Add the sit cue when you know you can get the behavior. Your dog doesn't know what the word means until you repeatedly associate it with the appropriate behavior.
- When your Boxer sits easily on cue, start using intermittent reinforcement by clicking some sits but not clicking others. At first, click most sits and skip an occasional one (this is a high reinforcement

rate). Gradually make your clicks more and more random.

DOWN: If your Boxer can sit, then he can learn to lie down.

◆ Have your Boxer sit.

◆ Hold the treat in front of his nose. Move it down slowly, straight toward the floor (toward his toes). If he follows all the way down, click and treat.

◆ If he gets stuck, move the treat down more slowly. Click and treat for small movements downward — moving his head a bit lower, or inching one paw forward. Keep clicking and treating until your Boxer is all the way down. This is called "shaping" — rewarding small pieces of a behavior until your dog succeeds.

◆ If your dog stands as you move the treat toward the floor, have him sit, and move the treat more slowly downward, shaping with clicks and treats for small movements down as long as he is sitting. If he stands, cheerfully say "Oops!" (which means "Sorry, no treat for that!"), have him sit and try again.

◆ If shaping isn't working, sit on the floor with your knee raised. Have your Boxer sit next to you. Put your hand with the treat under your knee and lure him under your leg so that he lies down and crawls to follow the treat. Click and treat!

◆ When you can lure the down easily, add the verbal cue, wait a few seconds to let your dog think, then lure him down to show him the association. Repeat until he'll go down on the verbal cue. Then begin using intermittent reinforcement.

STAY: What good are sit and down cues if your dog doesn't stay?

▲ Start with your Boxer in a sit or down position.

▲ Put the treat in front of your dog's nose and keep it there.

▲ Click and reward several times while he is in position, then release him with a cue that you will always use to tell him the stay is over. Common release cues are: "all done," "break," "free," "free dog," "at ease" and "OK."

▲ When your Boxer will stay in a sit or down position while you click and treat, add your verbal stay cue. Say "stay," pause for a second or two, click and say "stay" again. Release.

▲ When he's getting the idea, say "stay," whisk the treat out of sight behind your back, click and whisk the treat back.

Be sure to get it all the way to his nose, so he doesn't jump up. Gradually increase the duration of the stay.

▲ When your Boxer will stay for 15 to 20 seconds, add small distractions: shuffling your feet, moving your arms, small hops. Increase distractions gradually. If he

SMART TIP!

If you begin teaching the heel cue by taking long walks and letting the dog pull you along, she may misinterpret this action as an acceptable form of taking a walk. When you pull back on the leash to counteract her pulling, she will read that tug as a signal to pull even harder!

makes mistakes, you're adding too much, too fast.

▲ When he'll stay for 15 to 20 seconds with distractions, gradually add distance. Have your dog stay, take a half-step back, click, return and treat. When he'll stay with a half-step, tell him to stay, take a full step back, click and return. Always return to your dog to treat after you click, but before you release. If you always return, his stay becomes strong. If you call him to you, his stay gets weaker due to his eagerness to come to you.

COME: A reliable recall — coming when called — can be a challenging behavior to teach. It is possible, however. To succeed, you need to install an automatic response to your come cue — one so automatic that your Boxer doesn't even stop to think when he hears it, but will spin on his heels and charge to you at full speed.

■ Start by charging a come cue the same way you charged your clicker. If your Boxer already ignores the word "come," pick a different cue, like "front" or "hugs." Say your cue and feed him a bit of scrumptious treat. Repeat this until your Boxer's eyes

Once your Boxer understands what behavior goes with a specific cue, it is time to start weaning her off food treats. At first, give her a treat after each exercise. Then, start to give a treat only after every other exercise. Mix up the times when you offer a food reward and when you only offer praise. This way your dog will never know when she is going to receive food and praise or only praise.

light up when he hears the cue. Now you're ready to start training.

■ With your Boxer on a leash, run away several steps and cheerfully call out your charged cue. When he follows, click the clicker. Feed him a treat when he reaches you. For a more enthusiastic come, run away at full speed as you call him. When he follows at a gallop, click, stop running and give him a treat. The better your Boxer gets at coming, the farther away he can be when you call him.

■ Once your Boxer understands the come cue, play with more people, each with a clicker and treats. Stand a short distance apart and take turns calling and running away. Click and treat in turn as he comes to each of you. Gradually increase the distance until he comes flying to each person from a distance.

■ When you and your Boxer are ready to practice in wide-open spaces, attach a long line — a 20- to 50-foot leash — to your dog, so you can gather up your Boxer if that taunting squirrel nearby is too much of a temptation. Then, head to a practice area where there are less tempting distractions.

HEEL: Heeling means that your dog walks beside his owner without pulling. It takes time and patience on your part to succeed at teaching your dog that you will not proceed unless he is walking calmly beside you. Pulling out ahead on the leash is definitely not acceptable.

● Begin by holding the leash in your left hand as your Boxer sits beside your left leg. Move the loop end of the leash to your right hand, but keep your left hand short on the leash so that it keeps your dog close to you.

● Say "heel" and step forward on your left foot. Keep your Boxer close to you and take three steps. Stop and have the dog sit next to you in what we now call the heel position. Praise verbally, but do not touch the dog. Hesitate a moment and begin again with "heel," taking three steps and stopping, at which point the dog is told to sit again.

Your goal here is to have your dog walk those three steps without pulling on the leash. Once he will walk calmly beside you for three steps without pulling, increase the

Be consistent in your verbal cues so your Boxer will learn to understand them.

NOTABLE & QUOTABLE

If you want to make your dog happy, create a digging spot where she's allowed to disrupt the earth. Encourage her to dig there by burying bones and toys, and helping her dig them up. — Pat Miller, a certified dog trainer and owner of Peaceable Paws dog-training facility in Hagerstown, Md.

number of steps you take to five. When he will walk politely beside you for five steps, you can increase the length to 10. Keep increasing the length until your dog will walk quietly beside you without pulling for as long as you want him to heel. When you stop heeling, indicate to your dog that the exercise is over by petting him and saying "OK, good dog." The "OK" is used as a release word, meaning that the exercise is finished, and he is free to relax.

● If you are dealing with a Boxer who insists on pulling you around, simply put on your brakes and stand your ground until your Boxer realizes that the two of you are not going anywhere until he is beside you and moving at your pace, not his. It may take some time just standing there to convince your dog that you are the leader, and you will be the one to decide on the direction and speed of your travel.

● Each time the dog looks up at you or slows down to give slack between the two of you, quietly praise him and say, "Good heel. Good dog." Eventually, your Boxer will begin to respond, and he will be walking politely beside you without pulling on the leash. At first, the training sessions should be kept short and very positive; soon the dog will be able to walk nicely with you for increasingly longer distances. Remember to give your dog free time and the opportunity to run and play when you have finished heel practice.

SMART TIP!

It's a good idea to enroll your Boxer in an obedience class if one is available in your area. Many areas have dog clubs that offer basic obedience training and preparatory classes for obedience competition. There are also local dog trainers who offer similar classes.

LEAVE IT ALONE

Boxers enjoy eating, which makes it easy to train them using treats. But there's a downside to their gastronomic gusto — some Boxers gobble down anything even remotely edible. This could include fresh food, rotten food, things that once were food and any item that's ever been in contact with food. So, if you don't want your Boxer gulping ground trash, teach him to leave things alone when told.

■ Place a tempting tidbit on the floor, and cover it with your hand (gloved against teeth, if necessary). Say your cue word ("Leave it" or "Nah").

Your Boxer might lick, nibble and paw your hand; don't give in to him or you'll be rewarding his bad manners.

■ Wait until dog moves away, then click or praise and give him a treat. Do not let the dog eat the temptation food that's on the floor, only the treats you give him. Repeat until dog stops moving toward the food temptation.

NOTABLE & QUOTABLE

Most new owners are not prepared for the extent of their Boxer's energy level, and this is the root of many common problems: jumping, leash pulling, wild and destructive behavior — even some forms of aggression. There is a very simple and effective solution to this: exercise, exercise, exercise!

— longtime Boxer owner and obedience competitor Yogi Cutitta of Salem, Mass.

The best way to get your Boxer well-socialized is to introduce her to different kinds of people and situations. Go online to download a socialization checklist at **DogChannel.com/Club-Boxer**

■ Lift your hand momentarily, letting your Boxer see the temptation. Say the cue word. Be ready to protect the treat but instantly reward your dog if he resists temptation. Repeat, moving your hand farther away and waiting longer before clicking and rewarding your Boxer.

■ Increase the difficulty gradually — practice in different locations, add new temptations, drop treats from a standing height, drop several at a time and step away.

Remember to use your cue, so your Boxer will know what's expected of him. Always reward good behavior! Rehearse this skill daily for a week. After that, you should have enough real-life opportunities to practice.

TRAINING TIPS

If not properly socialized, managed and trained, even well-bred Boxers will exhibit undesirable behaviors such as jumping up, barking, chasing, chewing and other destructive behaviors. You can prevent these annoying habits and help your Boxer become the perfect dog you've wished for by following some basic training and behavior guidelines.

Be consistent. Consistency is important, not just in relation to what you allow your Boxer to do (get on the sofa, perhaps) and not do (jump up on people), but also in the verbal and body language cues you use with your dog and in his daily routine.

Be gentle but firm. Positive training methods are very popular. Properly applied, dog-friendly methods are wonderfully effective, creating canine-human relationships based on respect and cooperation.

Manage behavior. All living things repeat behaviors that are rewarded. Behaviors that aren't reinforced will go away.

Provide adequate exercise. A tired dog is a well-behaved dog. Many behavior problems can be avoided, others resolved, by providing your Boxer with enough exercise.

THE THREE-STEP PROGRAM

Perhaps it's too late to give your dog consistency, training and management from the start. Maybe he came from a Boxer rescue or a shelter, or you didn't realize the importance of these tenets when he was a pup. He already may have learned some bad behaviors. Perhaps they're even part of his genetic package. Many problems can be modified with ease using the following three-step process for changing an unwanted behavior.

Step No. 1: Visualize the behavior you want from your dog. If you simply try to stop your Boxer from doing something, you leave a behavior vacuum. You need to fill that vacuum with something so your dog doesn't return to the same behavior or fill it with one that's even worse! If you're tired of your dog jumping up, decide what you'd prefer instead. A dog who greets people by sitting politely in front of them is a joy to own.

Step No. 2: Prevent your dog from being rewarded for behavior you don't want. Management to the rescue! When he jumps up to greet you or get your attention, turn your back and step away to show him that jumping up no longer works to gain attention.

Step No. 3: Generously reinforce the desired behavior. Remember, dogs repeat behaviors that reward them. If your Boxer no longer gets attention for jumping up and is heavily reinforced with attention and treats for sitting, he will offer sits instead of jumping, because sits get him what he wants.

COUNTER CONDITIONING

Behaviors that respond well to the three-step process are those where your dog does something in order to get good

stuff. He jumps up to get attention. He countersurfs because he finds goodies on counters. He nips at your hands to get you to play with him.

The three steps don't work well when you're dealing with behaviors that are based in strong emotion, such as aggression and fear, or with hardwired behaviors such as chasing prey. With these, you can change your dog's emotional or hardwired response through counter conditioning — programming a new emotional or automatic response to the stimulus by giving it a new association. Here's how you would counter condition a Boxer who chases after skateboarders when you're walking him on a leash.

1. Have a large supply of very high-value treats, such as canned chicken.

2. Station yourself and your leashed Boxer where skateboarders will pass by at a subthreshold distance X — that is, where your dog alerts but doesn't lunge and bark.

3. Wait for a skateboarder. The instant your Boxer notices the skateboarder, feed him bits of chicken, nonstop, until the skateboarder is gone.

4. Repeat many times until, when the skateboarder appears, your Boxer looks at you with a big grin as if to say, "Yay! Where's my chicken?" This is a conditioned emotional response, or CER.

5. When you have a consistent CER at distance X, decrease the distance slightly, perhaps minus 1 foot, and repeat until you consistently get the CER at this distance.

6. Continue decreasing the distance and obtaining a CER at each of these distances, until a skateboarder zooming right past your Boxer's nose elicits the happy "Where's my chicken?" response. Now go back to distance X and add another zooming skateboarder. Continue this process of gradual desensitization until your Boxer does not turn a hair at a bevy of skateboarders racing by.

Even the best dogs have some bad habits. If you are frustrated with a particular behavior that your Boxer exhibits, don't despair! Go online and join Club Boxer where you can ask other Boxer owners for advice on dealing with excessive digging, stubbornness, housetraining issues and more. Log on to **DogChannel.com/Club-Boxer** and click on "Community."

JOIN OUR ONLINE **Club Boxer™**

BAD HABITS

Discipline — training one to act in accordance with rules — brings order to life. It is as simple as that. Without discipline, particularly in a group society, chaos reigns supreme and the group will eventually perish.

Humans and canines are social animals and need some form of discipline in order to function effectively. Boxers need discipline in their lives in order to understand how their pack (you and other family members) functions and how they must act in order to survive.

Living with an untrained Boxer is a lot like owning a piano that you don't know how to play; it is a nice object to look at but it doesn't do anything more than that to bring you pleasure. Now try taking piano lessons, and suddenly, the piano comes alive and brings forth magical sounds and rhythms that set your heart singing and your body swaying. The same is true with your Boxer. Any dog is a big responsibility and if not sensibly trained may develop unacceptable behavior that annoys you or could even cause family friction.

To train your Boxer, you should consider enrolling in an obedience class to teach him good manners as you learn how and why he behaves the way he does. Find out how to communicate with your dog and how to recognize and understand his communication with you. Suddenly, your dog takes on a new role in your life; he is smart, interesting, well-behaved and fun to be with. He demonstrates his bond of devotion to you daily. In other words, your Boxer does wonders for your ego because he constantly reminds you that you are not only his leader, you are his hero!

Those who teach dog obedience and counsel owners about their dogs' behavior have discovered some interesting facts about dog ownership. For example, training dogs when they are puppies results in the highest success rate in developing well-mannered and well-adjusted adult dogs. Training an older dog, from 6 months to 6 years of age, can produce almost equal results as long as the owner accepts the dog's slower learning rate and is willing to work patiently to help the dog succeed at developing to his fullest potential. Unfortunately, many owners of untrained adult dogs lack the patience necessary, so they do not persist until their dogs are successful at learning particular behaviors.

Training a puppy aged 10 to 16 weeks (20 weeks at the most) is like working with a dry sponge in a pool of water. The pup soaks up whatever you show him and constantly looks for more things to do and learn. At this early age, his body is not yet producing hormones, and therein lies the reason for such a high success rate. Without hormones, your pup is focused on his owners and not particularly interested in investigating other places, dogs, people, etc. You are his leader — his provider of food, water, shelter and security. He latches onto you and wants to stay close. He usually will follow you from room to room, will not let you out of his sight when you are outdoors with him and

will respond in like manner to the people and animals you encounter. If you greet a friend warmly, he will be happy to greet the person as well. If, however, you are hesitant, even anxious, about the approach of a stranger, he will respond accordingly.

Once the puppy begins to produce hormones, his natural curiosity emerges and he begins to investigate the world around him. It is at this time when you may notice that the untrained dog begins to wander away from you and even ignore your commands to stay close.

There are probably classes within a reasonable distance of your home, but you also can do a lot to train your dog yourself. This chapter is devoted to helping you correct some common bad habits that your Boxer may exhibit. If the recommended procedures are followed faithfully, you may expect positive results that will prove rewarding to both you and your dog.

Whether your new charge is a puppy or a mature adult, the methods of teaching and the techniques we use in training basic behaviors are the same. After all, no dog, whether puppy or adult, likes harsh or inhumane training methods. All creatures, however, respond favorably to gentle motivational methods, sincere praise and encouragement.

The following behavioral issues are the ones most commonly encountered by dog owners. Every dog and every situation is unique. Because behavioral abnormalities are the leading reason for owners' abandoning their pets, we hope that you will make a valiant effort to solve your Boxer's issues.

NIP NIPPING

As puppies start to teethe, they feel the need to sink their teeth into anything —

SMART TIP!

The golden rule of dog training is simple. For each "question" (cue), there is only one correct answer (reaction). One cue equals one reaction. Keep practicing the cue until your dog reacts correctly without hesitation. Be repetitive but not monotonous. Dogs get bored just as people do; a bored dog's attention will not be focused on the lesson.

unfortunately that includes your fingers, arms, hair, toes, whatever happens to be available. You may find this behavior cute for about the first five seconds — until you feel just how sharp those puppy teeth are.

Nipping is something you want to discourage immediately and consistently with a firm "No!" (or whatever number of firm "Nos" it takes for your dog to understand that you mean business) and replace your finger with an appropriate chew toy.

STOP THAT WHINING

A puppy will often cry, whine, whimper, howl or make some type of commotion when he is left alone. This is basically his way of calling out for attention, of calling out to

make sure that you know he is there and that you have not forgotten about him. He feels insecure when he is left alone; for example, when you are out of the house and he is in his crate, or when you are in another part of the house and he cannot see you. The noise he is making is an expression of the anxiety he feels at being alone, so he needs to be taught that being alone is OK. You are not actually training the dog to stop making noise, you are training him to feel comfortable when he is alone and thus removing the need to whine.

This is where the crate with a cozy blanket and a toy comes in handy. You want to know that your pup is safe when you are not there to supervise, and you know that he will be safe in his crate rather than roaming freely about the house. In order for your pup to stay in his crate without making a fuss, he needs to be comfortable in his crate. On that note, it is extremely important that the crate is never used as a form of punishment, or your pup will have a negative association with the crate.

Acclimate your pup to his crate in short, gradually increasing intervals of time in which you put him in the crate, maybe with a treat, and stay in the room with him. If he cries or makes a fuss, do not go to him, but stay in his sight. Gradually, he will realize that staying in his crate is all right without your help, and it will not be so traumatic for him when you are not around. You may want

Cratetraining helps curb bad behavior and aids in housetraining.

Your Boxer may howl, whine or otherwise vocalize her displeasure at your leaving the house and being left alone. This is a normal case of separation anxiety, but there are things that can be done to eliminate this problem. Your dog needs to learn that she will be fine on her own for a while and that she will not wither away if she isn't attended to every minute of the day.

In fact, constant attention can lead to separation anxiety in the first place. If you are endlessly coddling and cuddling your Boxer, she will come to expect this from you all of the time, and it will be more traumatic for her when you are not there.

To help minimize separation anxiety, make your entrances and exits as low-key as possible. Do not give your Boxer a long, drawn-out good-bye, and do not lavish her with hugs and kisses when you return. This will only make her miss you more when you are away. Another thing you can try is to give your dog a treat when you leave; this will keep her occupied, keep her mind off the fact that you just left and help her associate your leaving with a pleasant experience.

You may have to accustom your Boxer to being left alone in intervals, much like when you introduced her to her crate. Of course, when your dog starts whimpering as you approach the door, your first instinct will be to run to her and comfort her, but don't do it! Eventually, she will adjust and be just fine, if you take it in small steps.

Her anxiety stems from being placed in an unfamiliar situation; by familiarizing her with being alone she will learn that she is OK. When your Boxer is in the house alone, confine her in her crate or a designated dog-proof area. This should be the area in which she sleeps, so she will already feel comfortable there and this should make her feel more at ease when she is alone. This is just one of the many examples in which a crate is an invaluable tool for you and your Boxer, and another reinforcement of why your dog should view her crate as a happy place, a place of her own.

to leave the radio on softly when you leave the house; the sound of human voices can be comforting to him.

CHEW ON THIS

The national canine pastime is chewing! Every dog loves to sink his "canines" into a tasty bone, but most anything will do! Dogs need to chew to massage their gums, to make their new teeth feel better and to exercise their jaws. This is a natural behavior deeply embedded in all things canine. Our role as owners is not to stop chewing, but to redirect it to positive, chew-worthy objects. Be a smart Boxer owner and purchase proper chew toys for your dog, like strong nylon bones made for large dogs. Be sure that the devices are safe and durable because your dog's safety is at risk.

The best answer is prevention: That is, put your shoes, handbags and other appealing objects in their proper places (out of the reach of the growing canine mouth). Direct puppies to their toys whenever you see them tasting the furniture legs or the leg of your pants. Make a loud noise to attract the pup's attention, and immediately escort him to his chew toy and engage him with the toy for at least four minutes, praising and encouraging him all the while.

SMART TIP! **Do not carry your puppy to her potty area.** Lead her there on a leash or, better yet, encourage her to follow you to the spot. If you start carrying her, you might end up doing this routine for a long time and your puppy will have the satisfaction of having trained you.

NO MORE JUMPING

Jumping up is a dog's friendly way of saying hello! Some owners don't mind when their dog jumps up, which is fine for them. The problem arises when guests arrive and your dog greets them in the same manner — whether they like it or not! However friendly the greeting may be, the chances are that your visitors will not appreciate your dog's enthusiasm. Your dog will not be able to distinguish upon whom he can jump and whom he cannot. Therefore, it is probably best to discourage this behavior entirely.

Pick a cue such as "Off" (avoid using "Down" because you will use that for your dog to lie down), and tell him "Off" when he jumps up. Place him on the ground on all fours and have him sit, praising him the whole time. Always lavish him with praise and petting when he is in the sit position. That way you are still giving him a warm affectionate greeting, because you are as pleased to see him as he is to see you!

UNWANTED BARKING MUST GO

Barking is a dog's way of talking. It can be somewhat frustrating because it is not easy to tell what a dog means by his bark: Is he excited, happy, frightened, angry? Whatever it is that your dog is trying to say, he should not be punished for barking. It is only when barking becomes excessive, and when excessive barking becomes a bad habit, that the behavior needs to be modified.

If an intruder came into your home in the middle of the night and the dog barked a warning, wouldn't you be pleased? You would probably deem your dog a hero, a wonderful guardian and protector of the home. On the other hand, if a friend drops by unexpectedly and rings the doorbell and is greeted with a sudden sharp bark, you would probably be annoyed at your Boxer.

NOTABLE & QUOTABLE

Stage false departures. Pick up your car keys and put on your coat, then put them away and go about your routine. Do this several times a day, ignoring your dog while you do it. Soon his reaction to these triggers will decrease.

— *September Morn, a dog trainer and behavior specialist in Bellingham, Wash.*

But isn't it just the same behavior? The dog does not know any better … unless he sees who is at the door and it is someone he is familiar with, he will bark as a means of vocalizing that his (and your) territory is being threatened. While your friend is not posing a threat, it is all the same to your dog. Barking is his means of letting you know that there is an intrusion, whether friend or foe, on your property. This type of barking is instinctive and should not be discouraged.

Excessive habitual barking, however, is a problem that should be corrected early on. As your Boxer grows up, you will be able to tell when his barking is purposeful and when it is for no apparent reason. Eventually you will be able to distinguish your dog's barks and with what they are associated. For example, the bark when someone comes to the door will be different from the bark when he is excited to see you. It is similar to a person's tone of voice, except that the dog has to rely entirely on tone because he does not have the benefit of using words. An incessant barker will be evident at an early age.

There are some things that encourage a dog to bark. For example, if your dog barks nonstop for a few minutes and you give him a treat to quiet him, he believes that you are rewarding him for barking. He will associate barking with getting a treat, and will keep doing it until he is rewarded.

FOOD STEALING AND BEGGING

Is your dog devising ways of stealing food from your cupboards? If so, answer the following questions: Is your Boxer really hungry? Why is there food on the coffee table? Face it, some dogs are more food-motivated than

others; some dogs are totally obsessed by a slab of brisket and can only think of their next meal. Food stealing is terrific fun and always yields a great reward — food! Glorious food!

The smart owner's goal, therefore, is to make the "reward" less rewarding, even startling! Plant a shaker can (an empty can with a lid that contains coins) on the table so that it catches your pooch off-guard. There are other devices available that will surprise a dog when he is looking for a mid-afternoon snack. Such remote-control devices, though not the first choice of some trainers, allow the correction to come from the object instead of the owner. These devices are also useful to keep the snacking pooch from napping on forbidden furniture.

Just like stealing food, begging is a favorite pastime of hungry puppies with the same reward — food! Dogs quickly learn humans love that feed-me pose and that their selfish owners keep the good food for themselves. Why would humans make do on kibble when they can cook up sausages and kielbasa? Begging is a conditioned response related to a specific stimulus, time and place. The sounds of the kitchen, cans and bottles opening, crinkling bags and the smell of food preparation will excite your Boxer and soon the paws are in the air!

Here is the solution to stopping this behavior: Never give in to a beggar, no matter how appealing or desperate! You are rewarding the dog for sitting pretty, jumping up, whining and rubbing his nose into you by giving him that glorious food reward. By ignoring the dog, you will (eventually) force the behavior into extinction. Note that the behavior likely gets worse before it disappears, so be

sure there aren't any "softies" in the family who will give in to your dog every time he whimpers, "Please."

DIG THIS

Digging, which is seen as a destructive behavior to humans, is actually quite a natural behavior in dogs and their desire to dig can be irrepressible and most frustrating to owners. When digging occurs in your yard, it is actually a normal behavior redirected into something your dog can do in his everyday life. In the wild, a dog would be actively seeking food, making his own shelter, etc. He would be using his paws in a purposeful manner for his survival. Because you provide him with food and shelter, he has no need to use his paws for these purposes, so the energy that he would be using may manifest itself in the form of little holes all over your yard and flower beds.

Perhaps your dog is digging as a reaction to boredom — it is somewhat similar to someone eating a whole bag of chips in front of the TV — because they are there and there is nothing better to do! Basically, the answer is to provide your dog with adequate play and exercise so that his mind and paws are

occupied, and so that he feels as if he is doing something useful.

Of course, digging is easiest to control if it is stopped as soon as possible, but it is often difficult to catch a dog in the act. If your Boxer is a compulsive digger and is not easily distracted by other activities, you can designate an area on your property where it is OK for him to dig. If you catch him digging in an off-limits area of the yard, immediately bring him to the approved area and praise him for digging there. Keep a close eye on him so that you can catch him in the act; that is the only way to make your Boxer understand where digging is permitted and where it is not. If you take him to a hole he dug an hour ago and tell him "No," he will only understand that you are not fond of holes or dirt, or flowers. If you catch him while he is stifle-deep in your tulips, that is when he will get your message.

POOP ALERT!

Feces eating, *coprophagia*, is, to most humans, one of the most disgusting behaviors that their dog could engage in, yet to a dog it is perfectly normal. Vets have found that diets with a low digestibility, containing relatively low levels of fiber and high levels of starch, increase coprophagia. Therefore, high-fiber diets may decrease the likelihood of your dog eating feces. To discourage this behavior, feed food that is nutritionally complete and in the proper amount. If changes in his diet do not seem to work, and no medical cause can be found, you will have to modify the behavior through environmental control before it becomes a habit.

There are some tricks you can try, such as adding an unpleasant-tasting substance to the feces to make them unpalatable or adding something to your dog's food which will make it taste unpleasant after it passes through your dog. The best way to prevent your dog from eating his stool is to make it unavailable; clean up after he eliminates and remove any stool from the yard. If it is not there, he cannot eat it.

Never reprimand the dog for eating stool, as this rarely impresses the dog. Vets recommend distracting the dog while he is in the act of stool eating. Another option is to muzzle the dog when he is in the yard to relieve himself; this usually is effective within 30 to 60 days. Coprophagia most frequently seen in pups 6 to 12 months of age, and usually disappears around the dog's first birthday.

AGGRESSION

This is the most obvious problem that concerns Boxer owners. Aggression can be a very big problem in dogs, but more so in a dog with a fighting background. Aggression, when not controlled, always becomes dangerous. An aggressive dog, no matter his size, may lunge at, bite or even attack a person or another dog. Aggressive behavior is not to be tolerated. It is more than just inappropriate behavior; it is not safe. It is painful for a family to watch their dog become unpredictable in his behavior to the point where they are afraid of him.

While not all aggressive behavior is dangerous, growling, baring teeth, etc., can be frightening. It is important to ascertain why the dog is acting in this manner. Aggression is a display of dominance, and the dog should not have the dominant role in his pack, which is, in this case, your family.

It's important not to challenge an aggressive dog as this could provoke an attack. Observe your Boxer's body language. Does he make direct eye contact and stare? Does he try to make himself as large as possible: ears pricked, chest out, neck arched? Height and size signify authority in a dog pack — being taller or "above" another dog literally means that he is "above" in the social status. These body signals tell you that your Boxer thinks he is in charge, a problem that needs to be addressed. An aggressive dog is unpredictable: You never know when he is going to strike and what he is going to do. You cannot understand why a dog that is playful and loving one minute is growling and snapping the next.

The best solution is to consult a behavioral specialist, one who has experience with Boxers if possible. Together, perhaps you can pinpoint the cause of your dog's aggression and do something about it. An aggressive dog cannot be trusted, and a dog who cannot be trusted is not safe to have as a family pet. If, you find that your dog has become untrustworthy and you feel it necessary to seek him a new home with a more suitable family and environment, explain fully to the new owners all your reasons for rehoming the dog to be fair to all concerned.

AGGRESSION TOWARD DOGS

A dog's aggressive behavior toward another dog sometimes stems from insufficient exposure to other dogs at an early age. In Boxers, early socialization with other dogs

NOTABLE & QUOTABLE

The purpose of puppy classes is for puppies to learn how to learn. The pups get the training along the way, but the training is almost secondary.
— professional trainer Peggy Shunick Duezabou of Helena, Mont.

is essential. Boxers are not naturally aggressive toward other dogs; they have been bred down from a fighting dog to an excellent loving house dog. It is the breeder and owner's responsibility to curb and redirect any signs of aggression so that the dog can become an upright member of canine society.

If other dogs make your Boxer nervous and agitated, he will lash out as a defensive mechanism, though this behavior is thankfully uncommon in the breed. A dog who has not received sufficient exposure to other canines tends to believe that he is the only dog on the planet. The animal becomes so dominant he does not even show signs that he is fearful or threatened. Without growling or any other physical signal as a warning, he will lunge at and bite the other dog.

A way to correct this is to let your Boxer approach another dog when walking on-leash. Watch very closely and at the very first sign of aggression, correct your Boxer and pull him away. Scold him for any sign of aggression and praise him when he ignores or tolerates the other dog. Keep this up until he stops the aggressive behavior, learns to ignore the other dog or accepts other dogs. Praise him lavishly for his correct behavior.

DOMINANT AGGRESSION

A social hierarchy is firmly established in a wild dog pack. The dog wants to dominate those under him and please those above him; they know there must be a leader. If you are not the obvious choice for emperor, the dog will assume the throne! These conflicting innate desires are what a dog owner is up against when he sets about training his dog. In training a dog to obey cues, the owner is reinforcing that he is top dog in the "pack" and that the dog should, and should want to, serve his superior. Thus, the owner is suppressing the dog's urge to dominate by modifying his behavior and making him obedient.

An important part of training is taking every opportunity to reinforce that you are the leader. The simple action of making your Boxer sit to wait for his food says that you control when he eats and that he is dependent on you for food. Although it may be difficult, do not give in to your Boxer's wishes every time he whines at you or looks at you with his pleading eyes. It requires constant effort to show your dog his place in the pack is at the bottom. This is not meant to sound cruel or inhumane; you love your Boxer and you should treat him with care and affection. You certainly did not get a dog just so you could boss around another creature.

Dog training is not about being cruel or feeling important, it is about molding the dog's behavior into what is acceptable and teaching him to live by your rules. In theory, it is quite simple: Catch him in appropriate behavior and reward him for it. Add a dog into the equation and it becomes a bit more trying, but as a rule of thumb, positive reinforcement is what works best.

With a dominant dog, punishment and negative reinforcement can have the opposite effect, making a dog fearful and/or act aggressively if he feels challenged. Remember, a dominant dog perceives himself at the top socially and will fight to defend his perceived status. The best way to prevent that is to never give him reason to think he is in control in the first place.

If you are having trouble training your Boxer and it seems as if he is constantly challenging your authority, seek the help of an obedience trainer or behavioral specialist. A professional will work with you and your dog to teach you effective techniques to use at home. Beware of trainers with excessively harsh methods; scolding is necessary occasionally, but the focus should always be on positive reinforcement.

If you can isolate what brings out fear, you can help your dog get over it. Supervise your Boxer's interactions with people and other dogs, and praise your dog when it goes well. If he starts to act aggressively in a situation, correct and remove him from the situation. Do not let people approach your dog and pet him without your expressed permission. That way, you can have the dog sit to accept petting and praise him when he behaves properly. Focus on praise and modifying his behavior by rewarding him when he acts appropriately. By being gentle and by supervising his interactions, you are showing him there is no need to be afraid or defensive.

SEXUAL BEHAVIOR

Dogs exhibit certain sexual behaviors that may have influenced your choice of male or female when you first purchased your Boxer.

To a certain extent, spaying or neutering will eliminate these behaviors, but if you are purchasing a dog who you wish to breed, you should be aware of what you will have to deal with throughout the dog's life.

Female dogs usually have two estruses per year with each season lasting about three weeks. These are the only times in which a female dog will mate, and she usually will not allow this until the second week of the cycle, but this does vary from female to female. If not bred during the heat cycle, it is not uncommon for a female to experience a false pregnancy, in which her mammary glands swell and she exhibits maternal tendencies toward toys or even other objects.

Boxer owners must recognize that mounting is not merely a sexual expression but also one of dominance. Be consistent and persistent and you will find that you can "move mounters."

CHAPTER 12

BOXERS LOVE

SPORTS

One of the best ways to ensure a good relationship with your dog is to become involved in an activity both of you can enjoy. A bored Boxer can easily become a troublesome Boxer. Every year volunteers place hundreds of Boxers turned in to rescue groups all across the country. Why? Lois Brooks, a rescue coordinator from Delaware, Ohio, says many owners are unprepared to deal with the high-energy level of the Boxer. "A Boxer needs a lot of interaction with his owner or family along with a great deal of exercise," she says. "If ignored, this breed can be 'imaginatively destructive.'" Becoming involved in an activity gives your Boxer a mental and physical outlet for excess energy while giving him one-on-one time with you.

Deciding what recreation or sport you and your Boxer would enjoy the most takes some consideration. Do you want a sport like agility where you and the dog are both active participants? Would you prefer an activity where the dog does most of the work, such as in scent training? Does something less physical such as visiting senior citizens sound more like your cup of tea? Perhaps a brief synopsis of some of the more popular dog-friendly recreations will help you narrow things down a bit.

Did You Know? The Fédération Internationale Cynologique is the world kennel club that governs dog shows in Europe and elsewhere around the world.

Before You Begin
Because of the physical demands of sporting activities, a Boxer puppy should not begin official training until she is done growing. That doesn't mean, though, that you can't begin socializing her to sports. Talk to your vet about what age is appropriate.

EXERCISE OPTIONS

All dogs need exercise to keep them physically and mentally healthy. An inactive dog is a fat dog, with the accompanying likelihood of joint strain or torn ligaments. Inactive dogs also are prone to mischief — and may do anything to relieve their boredom. This often leads to behavior problems, such as chewing or barking. Regular daily exercise such as walks and short play sessions will help keep your Boxer slim, trim and happy.

Provide your Boxer with interactive play that stimulates his mind as well as body. It's a good idea to have a daily period of one-on-one play, especially with a puppy or young dog. Continue this interaction throughout your dog's life, and you will build a lasting bond. Even senior dogs who are slowing down a bit need the stimulation that activity provides.

If your Boxer is older or overweight, consult your veterinarian about how much and what type of exercise he needs. Usually, a 10- to 15-minute walk once a day is a good start. As the pounds start to drop off, your dog's energy level will rise and you can increase the amount of daily exercise.

Whether a dog is trained in the structured environment of a class or alone with his owner at home, there also are many sporting activities that can bring fun and rewards to owner and dog once they have mastered basic obedience training.

OBEDIENCE TRIALS

Obedience trials in the United States trace back to the early 1930s, when organized obedience training was developed to demonstrate how well dogs and owners could work together. The pioneer of obedience trials was Helen Whitehouse Walker, a Standard Poodle fancier, who designed a series of exercises modeled after the Associated Sheep, Police and Army Dog Society of Great Britain. Since then, obedience trials have grown by leaps and bounds, and today more than 2,000 trials are held in the United States every year, with more than 100,000 dogs competing. Any registered American Kennel Club, United Kennel Club or Indefinite Listing Privilege dog can enter an obedience trial, regardless of conformational disqualifications or neutering.

Obedience trials are divided into three levels of progressive difficulty. At the Novice level, dogs compete for the Companion Dog title; at the Open level, dogs compete for a Companion Dog Excellent title; and at the Advanced level, dogs compete for a Utility Dog title. Levels are subdivided into "A" (for beginners) and "B" (for more experienced handlers). A perfect score at any level is 200, and a dog must score 170 or better to earn a "leg," three of which are needed to earn the title. To earn points, your dog must score more than 50 percent of the available points in each exercise; the possible points range from 20 to 40.

Once your dog has earned the UD title, he can compete with other proven obedience dogs for the coveted title of Utility Dog Excellent, which requires that your dog win "legs" in 10 shows. In 1977, the title

NOTABLE &
QUOTABLE

Once Boxers are trained, they are generally very reliable and consistent. If we give our Boxers what they need — kind, consistent training and plenty of exercise — their exuberance and energy become a delightful part of who they are.

— longtime Boxer owner and obedience competitor Yogi Cutitta of Salem, Mass.

Obedience Trial Champion was established by the AKC. Utility Dogs who earn legs in Open B and Utility B earn points toward their Obedience Trial Champion title. To become an OTCH, a dog needs to earn 100 points, which requires three first places in Open B and Utility under three different judges.

The Grand Prix of obedience trials, the AKC National Obedience Invitational, gives qualifying Utility Dogs the chance to win the newest and highest title: National Obedience Champion. Only the top 25 ranked obedience dogs, plus any dog ranked in the top three in his breed, are allowed to compete.

AGILITY TRIALS

Agility is one of the most popular dog sports out there. Training your Boxer in agility will boost his confidence and teach him to focus on you.

In agility competition, dog and handler move through a prescribed course, negotiating a series of obstacles that may include jumps, tunnels, a dog walk, an A-frame, a seesaw, a pause table and weave poles. Dogs who run through a course without refusing any obstacles, going off course or knocking down any bars, all within a set time, get a qualifying score. Dogs with a certain number of qualifying scores in their given division (Novice, Open, Excellent and Mach) at AKC trials, earn an agility title.

Several different organizations recognize agility events. AKC-sanctioned agility events are the most common. The United States Dog Agility Association also sanctions agility trials, as does the UKC. The rules are different for each of these organizations, but the principles are the same.

When your Boxer starts his agility training, he will begin by learning to negotiate each individual obstacle while on-leash as you guide him. Eventually, you will steer him

through a few obstacles in a row, one after another. Once he catches on that this is how agility works, he can run a short course off-leash. One day, you'll see the light go on in your Boxer's eyes as he figures out that he should look to you for guidance as he runs through the agility course. Your job will be to

tell him which obstacles to take next, using your voice and body as signals.

RALLY BEHIND RALLY

Rally is a sport that combines competition obedience with elements of agility, but is less demanding than either. Rally was designed keeping the average dog owner in mind, and is easier than many other sporting activities.

At a rally event, dogs and handlers are asked to move through 10 to 20 different stations, depending on the level of competition. The stations are marked by numbered signs, which tell the handler the exercise to be

performed at this station. The exercises vary from making different types of turns to changing pace.

Dogs can earn rally titles as they get better at the sport and move through the different levels. The titles to strive for are Rally Novice, Rally Advanced, Rally Excellent and Rally Advanced Excellent.

To get your Boxer prepared for rally competition, focus on teaching him basic obedience, for starters. Your dog must know the five basic obedience cues — sit, down, stay, come and heel — and perform them well before he's ready for rally. Next, you can enroll your dog in a rally class. Although he must be at least 6 months to compete in rally, you can start training long before his 6-month birthday.

CANINE GOOD CITIZEN

If obedience work sounds too regimented but you'd still like your Boxer to have a title, prepare him for the Canine Good Citizen test. This program is sponsored by the AKC, with tests administered by local dog clubs, private trainers and 4-H clubs.

To earn a CGC title, your Boxer must be well-groomed and demonstrate the manners that all good dogs should exhibit. The CGC test requires your dog to perform the sit, down, stay and come cues; react appro-

SMART TIP! If you find your dog isn't best suited for group activities, once you get your veterinarian's OK and basic obedience training behind you, you and your Boxer can also find plenty of opportunities for exercise, training and strengthening the bond between you in your own backyard.

priately to other dogs and distractions; allow a stranger to approach him; sit politely for petting; walk nicely on a loose lead; move through a crowd without going wild; calm down after play or praise; and sit still for examination by the judge. Rules are posted on www.akc.org or you can get more info at Club Boxer: Go to www.DogChannel.com/Club-Boxer and click "Downloads."

SCENT WORK

If you are hesitant to get your Boxer involved in scent work, think again. Cathy Markos of Mindoro, Wisc., has bred and competed in various sports with Boxers for many years. One of her Boxers, Dolly, has recently become a certified narcotics dog. Markos says proudly, "In just a short time on the job Dolly has already made a find that resulted in a felony drug charge against the offenders." Additionally, Markos is active in schutzhund, a sport that requires tracking as part of the training. The fact that four of her Boxers have schutzhund titles attests to the fact that Boxers can track. "Many a Boxer has the ability, energy and drive for scent work, including tracking," Markos says.

To teach your dog to use his nose, utilize such games as find-it and hide-and-seek. Begin by hiding a toy or treat where your Boxer can easily find it. At first, you may have to help until your dog gets the idea. For hide-and-seek, have someone hold your dog while you hide. As your dog gains proficiency in each game, gradually make the hiding places more obscure while offering less assistance, making your dog rely on using his nose to find you. Both games are beneficial and enjoyable.

To progress to tracking, lay a short, straight track with something rather odorous. Some trainers encourage dogs to stay on track by placing treats or toys along the

way. Tracks can gradually be made longer with integrated turns. This activity takes a great deal of canine concentration. While training, try to make sure your dog succeeds to help build his confidence. For standard competitive tracking events, your Boxer will be required to steadily follow and complete a human scent track in a large, open field. The more challenging variable surface tracking takes place over city-inspired terrain such as concrete, gravel and blacktop. Tracking is performed on an extended lead with no guidance or signals permitted from the handler. Just as in other events, progressive titles are increasingly difficult to earn.

Search and rescue is another activity that requires scent work. Although some organizations limit breed choice, many groups are less prejudicial. Not for the casual trainer, search-and-rescue work is demanding in regards to time investment, physical ability, first aid and even survival tactics. Air scenting, as well as tracking, is often required. To air scent a dog "casts" back and forth, sniffing the air for a lost person or a body. Unlike tracking, which is done on lead, air scenting is performed off-leash. This means your Boxer must be taught to ignore temptations such as squirrels and rabbits when working, a training feat in itself. Nevertheless, for those with the determination and skills,

NOTABLE & QUOTABLE

Boxers need a job to do. They need exercise, discipline and attention, in that order. They are working dogs; I make mine work for everything, even their meals. Doggie backpacks are great for diffusing hyperactivity. I have my dog carry a couple of water bottles. It focuses his mind and has a very calming effect. A long walk — 45 minutes to an hour — releases a dog's pent-up energy in a controlled manner. — Gary Berg of Boxer Angels Rescue in North Bellmore, N.Y.

Boxers must be taught early not to pull on the leash. Many are not given the appropriate amount of exercise so they are all full of energy. They also like to be out on the end of their leads taking charge and bossing everyone around.

there is no doubt search and rescue is one of the most gratifying endeavors you and your Boxer could undertake.

SCHUTZHUND

Originating in Germany, schutzhund involves three aspects of training: obedience, tracking and protection. The tracking and obedience portions are difficult enough, but without a doubt, what truly sets schutzhund work apart from other competitive events is the protection phase. In protection work your dog is taught to bite a human only on command from its handler or in the event that he, or his handler, is attacked. Your dog is required to respond to an "out" cue and immediately let go of the individual being bitten. A large dog has enough jaw pressure to break an unprotected arm, a sobering fact that illustrates the dedication required of the owner of a protection-trained dog.

Markos says the Boxer makes an excellent choice for schutzhund work. "Anyone wanting to become involved in schutzhund would do well to choose their Boxer carefully," she says. "Dogs bred strictly for show frequently do not have the drive and trainability necessary for this demanding sport. In Germany dogs must pass strict tests pertaining to temperament and working ability before they are bred. This is why so many schutzhund enthusiasts buy dogs bred from recent German lines."

In schutzhund, dogs are referred to as sharp or dull. Boxers are considered dull.

Dogs like to play, but the games they play with each other often include wrestling, biting and pawing. Inviting your Boxer to play with *you* might initially bring out some of those same kinds of natural rough tactics, so it's important to teach your dog to play with you following gentler rules.

A game of Thank You/Take It will teach your Boxer to gently take things you offer her and willingly release to you anything she has in her mouth.

Start with a tug toy or large plush toy that's big enough for you and your Boxer to each hold an end. Wiggle the toy to get your dog interested and offer it to her, saying "take it."

Continue to hold on and move your end of the toy playfully, while your dog chews and plays with her part. After a few moments, stop moving the toy and hold your hand still. With your other hand, offer your Boxer a yummy treat, about 6 inches from the side of her face, so she'll have to let go of the toy to turn her head toward the treat.

When you offer the treat, say "thank you." This will become your dog's cue to let go. She can't continue to grip the toy and also reach the treat, so she'll have to make a choice; she can hold onto the toy and miss out on the treat, or she can release the toy and eat the treat. If the treat is sufficiently enticing, most dogs quickly decide in favor of the treat. If she doesn't choose the treat, start again, using a less preferred toy and a more preferred treat. If she prefers toys to treats, offer her a second toy instead of a treat. When she lets go of the toy, continue to hold it where it was when she dropped her end.

As soon as she swallows the treat (or grabs the second toy), wiggle the original toy and say "take it." Continue holding your end, wait a few moments, then offer another treat as before, saying "thank you." Repeat this process five to 10 times, each time holding the treat a little farther from your dog's face.

When she's quickly releasing the toy to get the treat upon hearing the words "thank you," keep the treat close to you in a closed fist, so it's not visible to your dog. While she's holding the toy, say "thank you," and when she lets go, quickly open your treat hand and give her her reward.

When that step is going well, hand her the toy and say "take it," then release your end so your dog has full control of the toy. Let her play with it for a few moments, then take hold of it and say "thank you." Reward with several treats when she gives it to you, and then give the toy back to her, saying "take it." Always end the game by letting her keep the toy.

Once your dog learns this game you'll be able to ask her for anything she has in her mouth. If it isn't something she should have, reward her with a treat for giving it to you, then help her find a "legal" toy and play Thank You/Take It with that a few times, ending by letting her keep it.

Markos quickly points out that this is not an insult. "A sharp dog tends to be the type to bite first and ask questions later," she says. "A dull dog is more discriminating. It will think about a situation and then decide if a bite is really necessary rather than just exploding into action. Because of this, a protection trained Boxer is easier to live with than many other breeds."

THERAPY DOGS

Visiting nursing homes, hospices and hospitals with your Boxer can be a tremendously satisfying experience. Many times a dog can reach an individual who has otherwise withdrawn from the world. The people-oriented Boxer can be a delightful therapy dog. Rescue worker Lois Brooks says this breed seems to have an affinity for children that makes it a natural for visiting children in hospitals or mental-care facilities. Although a gentle nature is a plus, often the normally rambunctious dog seems to instinctively become gentler when introduced to those who are weak or ailing. Some basic obedience is, of course, necessary for therapy dogs and a repertoire of tricks is a definite plus. The sight of a clownish Boxer "hamming it up" can help brighten most anyone's day.

Most facilities require a dog to have certification from a therapy dog organization. Therapy Dog International and the Delta Society are two certification organizations. Generally speaking, if your dog can pass a Canine Good Citizen test, earning certification will not be difficult. Certified therapy dog workers frequently get a group together and regularly make visitations in their area.

SHOW DOGS

When you purchase your Boxer puppy, you must make it clear to the breeder whether you want one as just a lovable companion and pet, or if you hope to be buying a Boxer with show prospects. No reputable breeder will sell you a puppy and tell you that the dog will definitely be show quality because so much can change during the early months of a puppy's development. If you do plan to show, what you hopefully will have acquired is a puppy with show "potential."

To the novice, exhibiting a Boxer in the ring may look easy, but it takes a lot of hard work and devotion to win at a show such as the Westminster Kennel Club dog show — not to mention a little luck, too!

The first concept that the canine novice learns when watching a dog show is that each dog first competes against members of his own breed. Once the judge has selected the best member of each breed (Best of Breed) the chosen dog will compete with other dogs in its group. Finally, the dogs chosen first in each group will compete for Best In Show.

The second concept that you must understand is that dogs are not compared against one another. The judge compares each dog against the breed standard, the written description of the ideal specimen approved by the AKC. While some early breed standards were indeed based on specific dogs who were famous or popular, many dedicated enthusiasts say that a perfect specimen as described in the standard has never walked into a show ring, has never been bred and, to the woe of dog breeders around the globe, does not exist. Breeders attempt to get as close to this ideal as possible with every litter, but theoretically the "perfect" dog is so elusive, it is impossible. (Even if the perfect Boxer were born, breeders and judges probably would never agree that he was indeed the perfect representative of the breed.)

If you are interested in exploring the world of conformation, your best bet is to join your local breed club or the national (or parent) club, the American Boxer Club. These clubs often host regional and national specialties and shows for Boxers only, which can include conformation as well as obedience and field trials. Even if you have no intention of competing with your Boxer, a specialty is a like a festival for lovers of the breed who congregate to share on their favorite topic: Boxers! Clubs also send out newsletters, and some organize training days and seminars in order that people may learn more about their chosen breed. To locate the breed club closest to you, contact the AKC, which furnishes the rules and regulations for all of these events, plus general dog registration and other basic requirements of dog ownership.

To find more information about this popular dog breed, contact the following organizations. They will be happy to help you dig deeper into the world of Boxers.

American Boxer Club: This is the AKC-recognized breed club. The site lists Boxer information and provides support for owners, breeders and exhibitors. www.american boxerclub.org

American Kennel Club: The AKC website offers information and links to conformation, tracking, rally, obedience and agility programs and member clubs. www.akc.org

Canadian Kennel Club: Our northern neighbor's oldest kennel club is similar to the AKC in the states. www.ckc.ca

Heart of a Boxer Club: This site includes conformation, agility, obedience, rescue and breeding information. www.hoabc.org

Love on a Leash: There are more than 900 members of this pet-therapy organization. www.loveonaleash.org

National Association of Professional Pet Sitters: When you can't take your Boxer with you on trips, here's a resource you can count on. www.petsitters.org

it's a Fact

The **American Kennel Club** began registering dogs in 1884. It is America's oldest kennel club. The **United Kennel Club,** the second oldest, began registering dogs in 1898.

North American Dog Agility Council: This site provides links to clubs, obedience trainers and agility trainers in the United States and Canada. www.nadac.com

Therapy Dogs Inc.: Get your Boxer involved in therapy. www.therapydogs.com

Therapy Dogs International: Find more therapy dog info here: www.tdi-dog.org

United Kennel Club: The UKC offers several of the same events offered by the AKC. These events include agility, conformation and obedience. In addition, the UKC offers competitions in hunting and dog sport (companion and protective events). Both the UKC and AKC offer programs for juniors, ages 2 to 18. www.ukcdogs.com

United States Dog Agility Association: The USDAA has information on dog training, breed clubs, and events in the United States, Canada, Mexico and overseas. www.usdaa.com

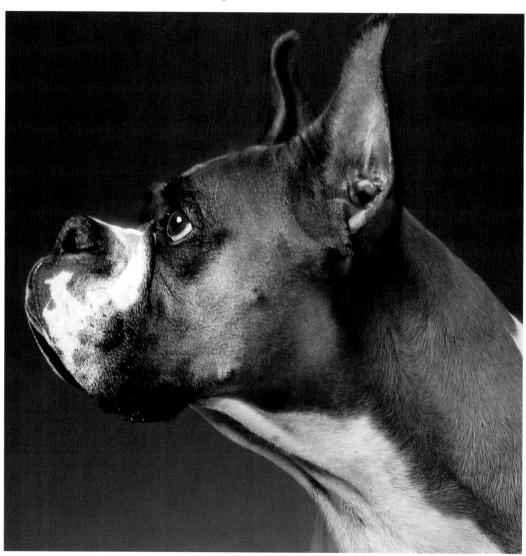

Going on a trip? Make sure to investigate the places you are visiting beforehand to see if dogs are allowed. Otherwise, you may have to board your Boxer.

BOARDING

So you want to take a family vacation — and you want to include all of the members of the family. You usually make arrangements for accommodations ahead of time anyway, but this is imperative when traveling with a dog. You do not want to make an overnight stop at the only place for miles around and find out that the hotel doesn't allow dogs. Also, you do not want to reserve a room for your family without confirming that you are traveling with a Boxer because, if it is against the hotel's policy, you may not have a place to stay.

Alternatively, if you are traveling and choose not to bring your Boxer, you will have to make arrangements for him. Some options are to bring him to a family member or a neighbor, have a trusted friend stop by often or stay at your house or bring your dog to a reputable boarding kennel.

If you choose to board him at a kennel, visit in advance to see the facilities and check how clean they are, and where the dogs are kept. Talk to some of the employees and see how they treat the dogs; do they spend time with the dogs, play with them, exercise them, etc.? Also find out the kennel's policy on vaccinations and what they require. This is for all of the dogs' safety because when dogs are kept together, there is a greater risk of diseases being passed from dog to dog.

HOME STAFFING

For the Boxer parent who works all day, a pet sitter or dog walker may be the perfect solution for the lonely Boxer longing for a midday stroll or a good game of fetch.

Dog owners can approach local high schools or community centers if they don't know of a neighbor interested in a part-time commitment. Interview potential dog walkers and consider their experience with dogs, as well as your Boxer's rapport with the candidate. (Boxers are excellent judges of character, unless there's liver involved.) Always check references before entrusting your dog, and opening your home, to a new dog walker.

For an owner's long-term absence, such as a business trip or vacation, many dog owners welcome the services of a pet sitter. It's usually less stressful on the dog to stay home with a pet sitter than to be boarded in a kennel. Pet sitters may also be more affordable than a week's stay at a full-service doggie day care.

Pet sitters must be even more reliable than dog walkers because the dog is depending on his surrogate owner for all of his needs for an extended period. Owners are advised to hire a certified pet sitter through the **National Association of Professional Pet Sitters**, which can be accessed online at **www.petsitters.org**.

NAPPS provides online and toll-free pet sitter locator services. The nonprofit organization only certifies serious-minded, professional individuals who are quite knowledgeable in canine behavior, nutrition, health and safety. Remember, always keep your Boxer's best interest at heart when planning a trip.

SCHOOL'S IN SESSION

Puppy kindergarten, usually open to dogs between 3 to 6 months, allows puppies to learn and socialize with other dogs and people in a structured setting. Classes help your Boxer enjoy going places with you, and help him become a well-behaved member at public gatherings that include other dogs. They prepare him for adult obedience classes, as well as for his life.

The problem with most puppy kindergarten classes is that they only occur one night a week. What about during the rest of the week?

If you're at home all week, you may be able to find other places to take your puppy, but you have to be careful about dog parks and other places where just any dog can go. An experience with a bully can undo all the good your classes have done, or worse, end in tragedy.

If you work, your puppy may be home alone all day, a tough situation for a Boxer. Chances are he can't hold himself that long, so your potty training will be undermined unless you're aiming to teach him to use an indoor potty. Chances are, by the time you come home, he'll be bursting with energy and you may start thinking that he's hyperactive.

The answer for the professional with a Boxer may be doggie day care. Most larger cities have some sort of day care, whether it's a boarding kennel that keeps your dog in a run or a full-service day care that offers training, play time and even spa facilities. They range from a person who keeps a few dogs at his home to a state-of-the-art facility built just for dogs. Many of the more sophisticated doggie day cares offer webcams so you can see your dog throughout the day.

Things to look for:
- escape-proof facilities, including a buffer between the dogs and outer doors
- inoculation requirements for new dogs
- midday meals for young dogs
- obedience training, using reward-based methods
- safe and comfortable sleeping areas
- screening dogs for aggression
- small groups of similar sizes and ages
- toys and playground equipment, such as tunnels
- trained staff, with an adequate number to supervise the dogs (no more than 10 to 15 dogs per person)
- a webcam

SMART TIP!

Remember to keep your dog's leash slack when interacting with other dogs. It is not unusual for a dog to pick a few canine neighbors to dislike. If you know there's bad blood, step off to the side and put a barrier, such as a parked car, between the dogs. If there are no barriers to be had, move to the side of the walkway, cue your dog to sit, stay and watch you until her nemesis passes; then continue your walk.

CAR TRAVEL

You should accustom your Boxer to riding in a car at an early age. You may or may not take him in the car often, but at the very least he will need to go to the vet, and you do not want these trips to be traumatic for your dog or troublesome for you.

The safest way for your dog to ride in the car is in his crate. If he uses a crate in the house, you can use the same crate to travel safely.

Another option is a specially made safety harness for dogs, which straps your Boxer in the car much like a seat belt. Do not let your dog roam loose in the vehicle; this is very dangerous! If you should stop short, your dog can be thrown and injured.

If your Boxer starts climbing on you and pestering you while you are driving, you will not be able to concentrate on the road. It is an unsafe situation for everyone — human and canine alike.

For long trips, stop often to let your Boxer relieve himself. Take along whatever you need to clean up after him, including some paper towels should he have an accident in the car or suffer from motion sickness.

IDENTIFICATION

Your Boxer is your valued companion and friend. That is why you always keep a close eye on him, and you have made sure that he cannot escape from the yard or wriggle out of his collar and run away from you. However, accidents can happen and there may come a time when your dog unexpectedly gets separated from you. If this should occur, the first thing on your mind will be finding him. Proper identification, including an ID tag, a tattoo and possibly a microchip, will increase the chances of his being returned to you safely and quickly.

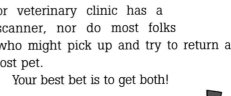

An ID tag on a collar or harness is the primary means of pet identification (ID licenses are required in many communities, anyway). Although inexpensive and easy to read, collars and ID tags can come, or be taken, off.

A microchip doesn't get lost. Containing a unique ID number which can be read by scanners, the microchip is embedded underneath a dog's skin. It's invaluable for identifying lost or stolen pets. However, to be effective, the microchip must be registered in a national database, smart owners will be sure their contact info is kept up-to-date. Additionally, not every shelter or veterinary clinic has a scanner, nor do most folks who might pick up and try to return a lost pet.

Your best bet is to get both!

Did You Know?

Some communities have created regular dog runs and separate spaces for small dogs. These small dog runs are ideal for introducing puppies to the dog park experience. The runs are smaller, the participants are smaller and their owners are often more vigilant because they are used to watching out for their fragile companions.

INDEX

BOXER, a Smart Owner's Guide™

part of the Kennel Club Books® Interactive Series™

LIBRARY OF CONGRESS CATALOGING-IN-PUBLICATION DATA

Boxer / from the editors of Dog fancy magazine.
　　　p. cm. — (Smart owner's guide)
　　Includes bibliographical references and index.
　　ISBN 978-1-59378-765-3
　1. Boxer (Dog breed)　I. Dog fancy (San Juan Capistrano, Calif.)

SF429.B75B625 2009
636.73—dc22

2009029701

JOIN
Club Boxer™
TODAY!